Solving *Behavior* Problems in Math Class

Academic, Learning, Social, and Emotional Empowerment

Grades K-12

Jennifer Taylor-Cox, Ph.D.

EYE ON EDUCATION
6 DEPOT WAYWEST, SUITE 106
LARCHMONT, NY 10538
(914) 833–0551
(914) 833–0761 fax
www.eyeoneducation.com

A sincere effort has been made to supply the identity of those who have created specific strategies. Any omissions have been unintentional.

Library of Congress Cataloging-in-Publication Data

Taylor-Cox, Jennifer.
  Solving behavior problems in math class : academic, learning,
social, and emotional empowerment / by Jennifer Taylor-Cox.
    p. cm.
  ISBN 978-1-59667-160-7
  1. Mathematics--Study and teaching. 2. Classroom management.
3. School discipline. I. Title.
  QA11.2.T39 2011
  510.71--dc22

                                              2010023138

10 9 8 7 6 5 4 3 2 1

Production services provided by
Rick Soldin a Book/Print Production Specialist
www.book-comp.com

Also Available from Eye On Education

Math Intervention:
Building Number Power with Formative Assessments,
Differentiation and Games, Grades 3-5
Jennifer Taylor-Cox

Math Intervention:
Building Number Power with Formative Assessments,
Differentiation and Games, Grades PreK-2
Jennifer Taylor-Cox

Family Math Night: Math Standards in Action
Jennifer Taylor-Cox

Family Math Night: Middle School Math Standards in Action
Jennifer Taylor-Cox and Christine Oberdorf

Mathematics Coaching Handbook:
Working With Teachers to Improve Instruction
Pia M. Hansen

Engaging Mathematics Students Using Cooperative Learning
John D. Strebe

Differentiated Instruction for K-8 Math and Science:
Activities and Lesson Plans
Mary Hamm and Dennis Adams

**Differentiated Assessment in Middle and
High School Mathematics and Science**
Sheryn Spencer Waterman

Teaching, Learning, and Assessment Together:
Reflective Assessments for Middle and
High School Mathematics and Science
Arthur K. Ellis and David W. Denton

Assessing Middle and High School Mathematics and Science:
Differentiating Formative Assessment
Sheryn Spencer Waterman

Mathematics and Multi-Ethnic Students: Exemplary Practices
Yvelyne Germaine-McCarthy and Katharine Owens

Contents

About the Author

Dr. Jennifer Taylor-Cox is an enthusiastic, captivating presenter, and well-known educator representing Taylor-Cox Instruction, LLC. Jennifer serves as a consultant in mathematics education and classroom behavior/discipline providing professional development opportunities for elementary, middle school, and high school educators in numerous districts across the United States. Her keynote speeches, professional development workshops, strategic coaching models, classroom demonstration lessons, study groups, and parent workshops are always high-energy and insightful.

Jennifer earned her Ph.D. from the University of Maryland and was awarded the Outstanding Doctoral Research Award from the University of Maryland and the Excellence in Teacher Education Award from Towson University. She served as the president of the Maryland Council of Teachers of Mathematics. Jennifer is the author of numerous professional articles and educational books.

Jennifer knows how to make learning mathematics engaging and meaningful, motivating learners of all ages! She has a passion for using formative assessments to differentiate math instruction and solve classroom behavior issues. With her deep understanding of how to connect research and practice in education, her zeal for improving the quality of education is alive in her work with educators, students, and parents. Jennifer lives and has her office in Severna Park, Maryland, and is the mother of three children.

If you are interested in learning more about the professional development opportunities Dr. Taylor-Cox offers, please contact her at **www.Taylor-CoxInstruction.com** or 410.729.5599.

Connecting Research and Practice in Education

Acknowledgements

This book is lovingly dedicated to Rev. Sandy S. W. Taylor, my first teacher.
Sincere appreciation is extended to an excellent group of reviewers.
Thank you for offering your encouragement and expertise.

Christine Oberdorf	Math Support Teacher, Montgomery County Public Schools
Edward C. Nolan	Mathematics Department Chairperson, Albert Einstein High School
Marci Goldman-Frye, M.S.	Mathematics Specialist, Montgomery County Public Schools
Bill Barnes	Coordinator of Secondary Mathematics, Howard County Public Schools
Aimee Domire	Teacher, New Hampshire Estates Elementary School
Shirley Sneed	Staff Development Teacher, Montgomery County Public Schools
Louis P. Albrecht	MCPO, Ret. U.S. Navy
Patricia Ziff	Faculty, Mount de Sales Academy

Gratitude is expressed to Marida Hines,
a talented and very creative illustrator.

Believe in the power of math!

Jennifer Taylor-Cox

Introduction

You may ask, "Why math class?" I recognize that behavior problems can happen in any class and the problems and solutions presented in this book could be applied to any class or subject. But we need to begin somewhere—and math *is* the most important subject, right math educators?

In all seriousness, this book is intended to focus on real problems in real math classrooms. The names have been changed, but each scenario represents a reoccurring problem that I have witnessed or situations that teachers have shared with me over the years. While these are not the only behavior problems that need to be solved in math class, they are some of the more frequent issues.

Chapter one begins with a bit of history about classroom discipline and a synthesis of much of the available literature on the topic. Chapter two offers a new perspective that involves empowering students in four important ways. Academic empowerment is the key, supported by learning empowerment, social empowerment, and emotional empowerment. Chapters three and four present actual behavior problems in math classrooms as well as solutions. Although these scenarios are presented in elementary (chapter three) or secondary (chapter four) settings, it is important to recognize that some classroom misbehaviors are not restricted to a specific age group. For example, bullies can be found in elementary, middle, and high schools. Likewise, misbehaviors transcend gender, race, and culture. The scenarios presented in this book are not intended to stereotype in any way. The goal is to look at specific misbehaviors and provide productive solutions. Chapter five concludes with several "smart moves" along with preventing behavior problems, monitoring progress, and making adjustments.

Meet the cast of math class characters

Tonya Tantrum

Tonya throws temper tantrums when she does not get her way. Find out what she does during a geometry lesson and learn how the teacher academically and emotionally empowers Tonya.

Raymond the Runner

Raymond darts out of the classroom and out of the school at any given time. He is known as the school's flight risk. Find out what he does during a number sense lesson and how the teacher addresses his academic and social issues to empower him.

Screaming Scott

Scott goes into a screaming fit several times a day. Find out what he does during an algebra lesson on patterns and how the teacher used academic and learning empowerment to help Scott.

Booker the Bully

Booker verbally threatens and taunts other students. And, he enjoys the chaos that erupts when he passes gas. Find out what he does during a unit on subtraction (with and without regrouping) and learn what the teacher does to increase Booker's academic and emotional empowerment.

Lizbeth the Lifter

Lizbeth likes to take things that do not belong to her. She seeks attention in inappropriate ways. Find out what happens during a lesson on graphing and how the teacher helps Lizbeth become academically and socially empowered.

Disinterested Diondre

Diondre acts as if he does not care about anything. He will do only the bare minimum of what is required even though he is a very capable student. Find out what happens during a unit on area and perimeter and how the teacher empowers Diondre by addressing his academic and learning needs.

Mouthy Maria

Maria talks back and acts sassy. She thinks she knows everything. Find out what happens when she argues with the teacher during a lesson on fractions. Learn how the teacher helped Maria increase her academic and emotional empowerment.

Daydreamer Dewain

Dewain never completes his homework and has trouble focusing in Algebra I. Find out what the teacher does to increase academic and learning empowerment to help Dewain be more successful.

Texting Tashi

Tashi sends text messages during her Algebra II class and insults the teacher. Find out what the teacher does to avoid power struggles and solve the behavior problems by academically and socially empowering Tashi.

Felix the Fighter

Felix fights, threatens his peers, and often cuts his General Education Math class. Find out what happens when Felix arrives to class ticked off. Learn how the teacher helps Felix increase his academic and emotional empowerment.

Rude Rashanda

Rashanda acts rude and angry. She uses foul language and fights with the teacher. Find out what happens when she leaves her geometry class and how the teacher learns to help Rashanda be successful through academic and emotional empowerment.

Carlos the Clown

Carlos thinks he is funny. He is the class clown in his trigonometry class. He seeks attention in inappropriate ways and roams the hallways looking for his friends. Find out what the teacher does to give Carlos academic and learning empowerment.

Sleepy Susanna

Susanna sleeps through most of her AP Statistics class. Find out why she is bored and what the teacher does to change the environment to provide Susanna with academic and learning empowerment.

Arrogant Anna

Anna acts like an entitled diva. She is talkative and suspected of cheating. Find out what happens when Anna insults her calculus teacher. Learn what her teacher does to improve the situation by providing academic and emotional empowerment.

1

The Past

The art of teaching is complex. We have so many distractions in our classrooms. Some students come to us with enormous baggage that impedes the teaching-learning process. Behavior problems relate to classroom discipline. Discipline should not be viewed as an ugly word. Discipline comes from the word *disciple.* Discipline means teaching. The goal is to educate, and there are effective strategies that can and should be used to improve the instructional environment. We need to ask: Which strategies work? What do they accomplish? How and why do these strategies work? Which strategies do not work? Why are they not working? We need to implement classroom discipline based on the answers to these and other questions.

In my doctoral studies, I learned that there are literally thousands of "research" pieces on the topic of classroom discipline and parts of this chapter are taken directly from my literature review. Amidst the mixture of information of yore and present-day streams of inquiry, we find opinions, commentaries, prescriptions, tentative assumptions, redundancy, contradictions, testimonies, and rationales. Two major themes emerge: Theories of Blame and Theories of Remedy.

Theories of Blame

This conglomeration of literature offers reasons why students "misbehave" in class and typically attaches accusation, sometimes, even condemnation. Embedded within this mass of literature are six subcategories asserting diverse sources of deficiency and implied causality. These include (1) Students are to blame because they have inherent intentions that become classroom behavior problems; (2) Parents are to blame for student misbehavior because of faulty child-rearing practices; (3) Biochemical conditions are to blame because some students have medical reasons that explain the misbehavior; (4) Peer influence is to blame because of peer pressure and the desire some misbehaving students have to perform for their peers; (5) Educators are to blame for problematic classroom behavior because they lack expertise and/or have erroneous expectations; and (6) The curriculum is to blame because it does not meet the academic needs of the misbehaving student.

Should We Blame the Students? Some Say, "Yes."

Alfred Adler, whom I refer to as the grandfather of discipline research, offered us a framework for the study of classroom discipline. The goals of misbehavior that Adler (1930, 1938) identified, Dreikurs (1948, 1958, 1972) later refined, and many classroom discipline resources still use today, offer teachers the reasons that children misbehave. According to the Adler-Dreikurs model, students have problems behaving appropriately because they successively seek attention, power, revenge, and pity (Dreikurs, 1972).

The following scenario is an example of a student moving through the complete Adler-Dreikurs model. See Figure 1.1.

Figure 1.1

Attention
Instead of completing his class work, Alex makes random bird calls while sitting at his desk.

Power
The teacher ignores Alex's noises. Therefore, Alex convinces a few other students to join him in making bird calls.

Revenge
The teacher yells at Alex to make him stop distracting the class. When the teacher turns her back to walk back to her desk, Alex holds up his middle finger at her.

Pity
Upon hearing the gasps from the class, the teacher says aloud, "Alex, I will see YOU in detention!" Alex can't believe he is the only one who has to go to detention. Other students were making bird calls and THEY did not get detention. He wonders why the teacher hates him so much.

Unfortunately, this type of situation plays out in many classrooms. Some students seek these goals of misbehavior. Other students do not successively move through all of the goals. Still other students misbehave for different reasons.

Yet, simply blaming the students does little to solve behavior problems in math class.

Should We Blame the Parents? Some Say, "Yes."

Among the arrays of information that children absorb are the interactions of social beings in a particular setting, usually the home. They learn, at very young ages, how to gather attention, display needs and desires, and interact with or gain reaction from adults. Parents, a child's first teachers, respond to needs, desires, and curiosity in various ways. Children who exhibit intense behavior problems in school often come from homes characterized as highly stressful and live with adults who have difficult temperaments and/or who lack adequate parenting skills (Patterson, Reid, & Dishion, 1992). Bearing in mind that students spend the majority of their lives out of school, it is important to consider home environments, specifically parents (or those acting as parents), as potential influences and possible sources of student behavior problems, keeping in mind that some students who misbehave come from stable home environments with supportive parents.

Households that are characterized by high levels of aggression, malice, oppression, and vitriol are likely to produce children with dispositions that engage in these behaviors. The lines of the famous poem by Dorothy Law Nolte (1998) summarize the point: "If a child lives with criticism, he learns to condemn. If a child lives with hostility, he learns to fight."

Yet, simply blaming the parents does little to solve behavior problems in math class.

Should We Blame the Biochemical Conditions? Some Say, "Yes."

Biological factors may also help explain the behavior of children. While we have advanced beyond the testing and measuring of children's skulls to research biologically connected behavioral problems in children, many educational practitioners and researchers continue to turn to the field of medicine for answers to classroom behavior problems. Terms such as "defective students" and "maladjusted children" have been replaced by labels such as "emotionally disturbed," "socially impaired," and "behaviorally disabled." These new labels are often connected to medically diagnosed conditions such as ADD (attention deficit disorder), ADHD (attention deficit with hyperactivity disorder), and conduct disorder.

Compounding the issue of biochemically explained behavior is the fact that some students come to school medically undiagnosed or misdiagnosed. Many children have inhabited several classrooms prior to official, medical diagnosis of behavior-related conditions. Therefore, it is possible that in any given classroom there are a few students who may have a medical explanation for inappropriate behavior but have not yet received official diagnoses that identify a primary cause.

Yet, simply blaming biochemical conditions does little to solve behavior problems in math class.

Should We Blame the Peers? Some Say, "Yes."

Some students learn how to behave by observing their peers. The desire to be like others, particularly those marked "favorite" or otherwise socially promoted, is an intense force often referred to as *peer pressure*. "Our peer group is a relentless influence on our behaviors, regardless of age or societal role" (Kauffman, Mostert, Trent, & Hallahan, 1998, p. 96). Considering that students are continually reforming their own self perceptions through the eyes of others, it is not surprising that many students feel obligated to follow the often wayward directions of peers rather than adults.

Numerous classroom behavior problems can be described as peer performances. As the sideshows of disruption are reinforced by peer acceptance and oft times urged on by peer pressure, the classroom environment becomes one composed of copious, yet traceable problems with student behavior.

Yet, simply blaming the peers does little to solve behavior problems in math class.

Should We Blame the Educators? Some Say, "Yes."

Just as students vary in skill level, personality, and behavioral tendencies, school personnel do as well. Some teachers and administrators are particularly skilled educators and leaders, others are mediocre, and still others are less than adequate. These variations in educator expertise have been connected to classroom behavior problems.

Violent Schools—Safe Schools, a report to the National Institute of Education, revealed that there were higher rates of suspension in schools that employed teachers who had low expectations of students, demonstrated racial bias, and generally acted disinterested in students (Wu, 1980). In settings such as these, a self-fulfilling prophecy is likely to occur. The teacher expects some (or all) students to perform poorly in academics and to exhibit behaviors of misconduct. Consequently, the students conform to teacher expectations. As the Stephen Covey adage goes, *Argue for a weakness and it's yours!* (Covey, 1990). Teachers who anticipate and focus on negative teacher/student interactions and problems with classroom behavior are prone to participate in the like.

Yet, simply blaming the educators does little to solve behavior problems in math class.

Should We Blame the Curriculum? Some Say, "Yes."

Other in-school factors such as curricular decisions have been shown to have an effect on classroom behavior. Often students display misbehaviors when the curriculum has not adequately met individual needs. Perhaps the task given to the student is too easy, or too difficult. If the work is too easy, students may act up because they are bored. If the work is too difficult, students may act up because they are frustrated.

Yet, simply blaming the curriculum does little to solve behavior problems in math class.

Theories of Blame: An Eclectic Justification, a Tool, or a Conundrum?

The abundance of theories that attach blame and causality to student misbehavior offer educators, students, and the larger society explanations for student behavior problems in the classroom. The explanations, although not comprehensive or applicable to all students, often pave the way for excuses for educators not to address the complex problems of student misbehavior.

- ◆ If the problem resides at home, how can the school address the issue?

- ◆ If the child has a medical explanation for misbehavior, how can the classroom teacher change his behavior?

- ◆ Are some of the blame theories, however accurate or inaccurate they may be, used to justify and perpetuate the problems of student misbehavior in the classroom?

Herein lies the zenith of the conundrum; educators can serve as both culprits and victims of student misbehavior in the classroom. Instead of focusing on blame, we need solutions.

Theories of Remedy

The literature on classroom behavior and discipline packaged in numerous classroom discipline "remedies" is a conglomeration of theoretical reflections and prescriptive notations. These various programs can be clustered into three major categories. The first major classification involves theories and techniques associated with behavior modification. The second category is concerned with authoritarian rule in the classroom. The third classification encompasses communicative and community environments in the classroom.

Behavior Modification

The majority of classroom behavior programs address behaviorism theory and behavior modification techniques (Kohn, 1996; Slee, 1995). Dating back to the work of Edward Thorndike (1913), scientists have turned to the animal kingdom to find answers related to the behavioral tendencies of human beings. Although B. F. Skinner (1953) is typically credited for "operant conditioning," which is the basic premise behind behavior modification, it was Thorndike (1913) who conducted the ground work (Woolfolk & McCune-Nicolich, 1984). Thorndike's animals of choice were cats. Using boxes with removable bolts on the lids, he contained the cats until they could figure out how to dislodge the bolts to obtain freedom and food. Over time, the cats "learned" to quickly escape and were thus rewarded with food. Thorndike concluded that "any act that produces a satisfying effect will tend to be repeated in that situation" (Woolfolk & McCune-Nicolich, 1984).

Skinner (1953) pushed Thorndike's theory to the next level, which moved beyond basic "stimulus and response" to the deliberate choice of action (operant) and associated consequences. Using rats and pigeons to test his theory, Skinner created cages with small food dispensing devices. The subjects were conditioned to dispense the food (the rats pushed a bar and the pigeons pecked a disk). Skinner studied the effects of various consequences (e.g., no food dispensed, electric shock) on behavior. Using these and similar "scientific" experiments, educational psychologists established a framework for the study of human behavior, that is, behaviorism, also known as behavior modification.

Behaviorism is typically understood through an action (behavior or response) situated between two mediums. Something precedes the action and something follows the action. In light of the theory of operant conditioning, the provoking medium is referred to as the "antecedent" and the resulting medium is designated the "consequence" (Woolfolk & McCune-Nicolich, 1984). In the study of operant behavior, specific actions result in specific outcomes.

Typically, approaches to behavior modification focus on the consequences or operants associated with the behaviors of children. Educators are supplied with a host of possible consequences to link with student behavior in an attempt to change the behavior to what is desired by the teacher. These are the "bags of tricks" that have replaced the paddle and dunce caps of old (Dubelle, 1995). The range of possible teacher-dictated consequences falls under the specific prototypes of positive reinforcement (which includes rewards), negative reinforcement (which, contrary to public perception, does *not* include punishment), extinction, and punishment. Positive reinforcement and negative reinforcement are typically used to increase specific classroom behaviors, while punishment and extinction are usually employed to reduce specific classroom behaviors (Kauffman et al., 1998).

Reinforcement—increasing specific behaviors

Reinforcement is the method of using a repeated consequence to increase the regularity of a specific behavior. According to behavioral psychologists, a reinforcer is required to increase the frequency of an appropriate behavior. Likewise, if a student or students repeatedly display a specific misbehavior, then some type of reinforcement is perpetuating that behavior (Woolfolk & McCune-Nicolich,1985). Included in the reinforcement construct is the notion of consistency. Most discipline program packages make mention of consistency in teacher reaction or interaction to eliminate behavior problems and promote positive classroom climates. Because reinforcement involves frequency, consistency is a mandatory factor that has the potential to strengthen or negate teacher-established consequences.

Positive reinforcement is the presentation of a stimulus immediately following a specific behavior. The range of positive reinforcement possibilities used by teachers is nearly infinite. Educators tend to assume that stickers, praise, credit, smiley faces, A's, candy, free-play time, pats on the back, winks, and thumbs up signals serve to promote positive behavior in classrooms. The fallacy is that, according to the behavioral scientists, nothing is a positive reinforcer until it serves to reinforce a behavior. Therefore, one cannot be sure that a reward is a positive reinforcer until it actually produces the desired behavioral outcome. Moreover, the behavioral scientists assert that reinforcers only work if they are contingent solely upon the display of the behavior—which means that Johnny can never get a smile from the teacher or anyone else unless he has just displayed the specific behavior!

Some rewards are not reinforcers; most are not completely contingent; yet, "carrots" are used in a large majority of classrooms. Rewards, like punishments, require surveillance and produce temporary compliance (Kohn, 1996). While rewards are time consuming, costly (economically and emotionally), and do little to develop moral growth in students, prizes and praises top the lists of behavior techniques used in many classrooms. According to Kohn (1996), "Do this and you'll get that' is at the heart of countless classroom management programs, including some that energetically promote themselves as positive or enlightened" (p. 32).

Although rewards constitute a large portion of carrot-oriented notions of positive reinforcement, there are other more antagonistic types of positive reinforcement that are present in many classrooms. Reactions of laughter or anger or basic attention can serve as positive reinforcers for disruptive behavior. As Woolfolk and McCune-Nicolich (1984) recount, "without realizing it, many teachers help maintain problem behaviors by inadvertently reinforcing these behaviors" (p. 173). Positive reinforcement can serve to perpetuate a behavior, be the behavior good, bad, or indifferent.

Negative reinforcement involves the extraction or cessation of a disagreeable stimulus. The notion connected to negative reinforcement is that behavior is based on avoiding a certain, unpleasant situation. If a student misbehaves intending to be removed from a class to avoid a specific assignment, then it is the assignment, not the punishment of removal from class, which has served as a negative reinforcer. Likewise, suspension can serve as a positive reinforcer and a vehicle for avoidance. If the child is uncomfortable in the classroom, then the classroom itself serves as the negative reinforcer.

The most prevalent types of intentional negative reinforcement used by educators come in the form of coercion. Coercion involves the struggle for power and control by way of causing discomfort or anguish to another. The power struggle victor uses negative reinforcement to coerce the contender into compliance and is essentially positively reinforced because she received what was desired. Coercion involves using one's power to get what one wants. Teachers using coercion decide when and where there is a problem, who owns the problem, and what to do about the problem.

Punishments—attempts at ending specific behaviors

Punishment, unlike coercion, is not a negative reinforcer because it involves a decrease in behavior. Punishment is intended to stop specific behaviors and comes in two forms. A punishment can be "cost related" which involves the removal of highly regarded goods (i.e., privileges, time, prizes) and punishment can be related to "aversive consequences," which may involve castigation, segregation, or pain (e.g., scolding, time-out, detention, embarrassment; Kauffman et al., 1998). Both types of punishment are intended to cause the perpetrator to suffer.

While punishments may advance control over student behavior and elicit change in student behavior, punishment "can't possibly have an effect on that person's motives or values, on the person underneath the behavior"

(Kohn, 1996, p. 26). Moreover, argues Kohn (1993), punishing students can actually discourage them from thinking morally and ethically because there is little need to do so. The punishment or likely punishment bequeaths a blockade to real-life moral decision making.

Extinction—eliminating reinforcement

To eradicate misbehaviors from the classroom, some discipline "fix it" programs include extinction, that is, the elimination of reinforcement. The notion behind extinction is that "when a behavior no longer produces the desired effect (positive or negative reinforcement), it will eventually fade away (be extinguished)" (Kauffman et al., 1998, p. 55). Many of the behavior modification-laden behavior programs include extinction as a strategy to be employed by teachers. One of the presumptions associated with extinction is that the reinforcer can be identified and isolated. Another presumption is that the reinforcer can be terminated. Since extinction is a gradual, time-consuming process that often begins with an increase in degree and/or frequency of the behavior problem before there is a decrease (Kauffman et al., 1998), many educators become frustrated with extinction, although it is commonly included in behavior modification programs.

The flaws in behavior modification

Unfortunately for educators in search of the miracle antidote (or a tranquilizer for that matter), behavior modification does not cure all classroom behavior problems, nor does it pave the way to uninterrupted academic instruction. Behavior modification is mechanical and shortsighted.

Questions about behavior modification to consider:

♦ Should we train students the same way we train animals?

♦ Do behavior modification techniques help students develop ethical behavior?

♦ What are the long-term effects of behavior modification?

Authoritarian Rule in the Classroom

Traditional views of classroom behavior often involve the teacher as authoritarian, control-oriented leader, and manager. In this view, the teacher is the authority figure to whom students must obey or pay the price of noncompliance, be that the teacher's wrath or another punitive measure.

In the past, public school educators used corporal punishment to impose dominance and control, thereby establishing the authority of the teacher. Students who failed to comply with school rules were subjected to physical punishment. As many former students remember (myself included), teachers cracking knuckles with rulers and administrators "administering" paddlings and beatings were the order of the day for misbehaving students.

These and other punishments were used to ensure that students were fearful of what might happen if they chose noncompliance. Thus, the proclaimed intent of corporal punishment was that it would deter students from misbehaving (i.e., students would be afraid to misbehave in the classroom).

Along with fear, guilt is another student emotion necessary in the authoritarian approach to classroom discipline. As Dubelle (1995) notes, "whenever students become fearful or feel guilty with the thought of punishment educators might use, punishments seem to exercise *control* over students' behaviors" (p. 4). Compelling students to experience emotions of guilt and apprehension is a critical dimension of the authoritarian, control-oriented perspective.

Control theory

One of the contributions to this authoritarian leadership view is William Glasser's *control theory,* which has been altered and redefined over the last several decades. Glasser first worked with prisoners (*Reality Therapy,* 1965) and then applied his conclusions to the educational setting (*Schools without Failure,* 1969; *Control Theory,* 1985; *Control Theory in the Classroom,* 1986; *The Quality School: Managing Students without Coercion,* 1990). Initial renditions of his theory (1985) involved a "ten step," systematic approach to addressing classroom behavior problems. Glasser (1985) proposed that teachers establish rules with students and continually assess and adjust the guidelines and class structure. If misbehavior surfaces, the teacher is to discuss the problem with the student; the student is to identify the infraction and corresponding rule and decide upon a remedial strategy. If the misbehavior persists, the student is removed from the classroom (time-out or in-school or at-home suspension, depending on the severity of the offense).

In his later work *Control Theory in the Classroom,* Glasser (1986) totters away from his original authoritarian-laden approach toward a paradigm that can, according to Glasser, enable teachers to surpass stimulus-response orientations (behavior modification approaches), implement cooperative learning and, thus, in his view, improve classroom conditions. Strikingly similar to Maslow's (1970) hierarchy of needs and embellished with notions resembling Hertzberg's (1966) motivational drives, Glasser's (1986) control theory offers a reflective view of the behaviors, feelings, and motivations of educators and students. Because the actions chosen by individuals, according to Glasser (1986), are all related to the basic needs of survival—belonging, power, freedom, and fun—children and adults alike are working to satisfy one or more of these needs as they behave. The concept of power remains a constant force throughout the metamorphosis of Glasser's theory of control.

The blemishes in authoritarian rule

Authoritative approaches to classroom discipline pose several problems. The methodology focuses on domination, coercion, and punishment. Furthermore, Kohn (1996) contends, traditional authoritarian approaches "warp the relationship between the punisher and the punished" (p. 27). The student's relationship with the teacher involves notions of discomfort and fear, which are often cast by authoritarian advocates as notions of respect.

In the authoritarian method, "children behave out of fear...as a result they have no inner controls....Once the controllers' backs are turned, the controllees can run wild" (Sears & Sears, 1995, p. 3). Students who are part of a classroom environment that is dominated by teacher command are prone to misbehave whenever they are given the chance to do so. In this light, the authoritarian approach preserves the ill-fated behaviors by temporarily putting them on hold, rather than extinguishing them. Consequently, students learn when to "misbehave," rather than how to "behave appropriately."

Questions about authoritarian rule to consider:

- If fear is respect, then does mutual respect mean mutual fear?

- What are the long term educational and functional goals for students?

- Does forcing students to comply with teacher commands resemble animal training, rather than education?

- How far removed is the authoritarian approach from emotional and/or verbal abuse?

Communicative and Community-Oriented Remedies

Some classroom discipline programs depart from the authoritarian version of control theory and from behavior modification to focus on classroom community, communication, and student-directed conflict resolution. While it is often the teacher who initiates and guides the implementation of these techniques, the focal points are community, communication, and student-to-student reactions, interactions, and responsibilities. In these programs, it is the establishment of community, utilization of positive communication techniques, and the use of conflict resolution techniques in the classroom that serve to remedy problems with classroom behavior.

Abandoning subordination and inviting community

This view of approaching classroom behavior problems through inviting community involves a paradigm shift for educators. Disheartened by the over use of punishments and rewards in classrooms, many educators are beginning to build a different kind of classroom community, which includes continual evaluation of the curriculum and environment. Recognizing that rewards and punishments are only effective in securing short-term compliance, Kohn (1996) asserts that educators need to take an evaluative look at their long-term goals for students. In Kohn's (1996) approach, the alignment of goals and practices, constant evaluation, and the establishment of a communal environment are encouraged. Therefore, unlike behavior modification, theories of control, and the many discipline programs that are grounded by them, we need to shift the responsibility of change and success from the students *or* the educators to the students *and* the educators.

Communication and conflict resolution

Other scholars have worked with some of the same communicative notions of this perspective on classroom behavior. Hence, the focus is on how to strengthen classroom community by improving communication between and among students. This assembly of literature often comes in the form of conflict resolution models. In addition, many scholars promote creating a classroom environment that invites learning and positive social interactions. Often these ideas include using logical consequences, maintaining dignity, and encouraging students to have a positive attitude about the content.

Communication and community—synonymous?

While building a positive classroom community is a foundational component to successful discipline, student misbehaviors persist. Additionally, many conflict resolution models fall short of obtaining the proclaimed goals of solving problems and establishing community. While some students may learn to "talk it out," they may falter when it comes to listening to or understanding the perspectives of others. Other students may learn to appreciate the paradigms of others, but fail to make accommodations in their own behavioral tendencies.

At best, a successful conflict resolution enables students to learn verbal communication skills; but, do these communication skills translate into notions of classroom community?

- ◆ Are not teachers and students part of a community regardless of the use of verbal exchanges geared toward problem solving?

- ◆ What is community and how is it related to conflict resolution and classroom behavior?

Remedy theories: Sensible answers or more problems?

The theories of remedy aimed at solving classroom behavior problems carry a host of presumptions and potential problems. The techniques associated with behavior modification are perfunctory in nature. Training children to behave in a certain manner for the sole purpose of receiving a reward or avoiding a punishment fails to consider the fact that education involves more than learning simplistic cause/effect relationships. If, as Kohn (1996) highlights, educators are to enable children to "become morally sophisticated people who think for themselves..." (p. 62), then educators are doing an injustice to children by "teaching" them to perform (not far from the notion of training seals) through behavior modification techniques.

In like manner, the remedies to classroom behavior problems that involve an authoritarian rule in the classroom and the associated notions of control focus on dominating and coercing children into specific behaviors. Forcing children to behave out of fear teaches children to have "no inner controls" and to "run wild" when given the opportunity (Sears & Sears, 1995 p. 3). While methods of control and behavior modification can be successful means of achieving student compliance, the compliance may be at best temporary and at worst detrimental to the emotional and social growth of children (Kohn 1996).

Of the theories of remedy, the community and communicative-oriented approaches hold the greatest potential for addressing classroom behavior problems over the long haul. While some of the community-oriented approaches aspire to unrealistic ideals, and, while a majority of the conflict resolution models are too concerned with offering specific recipes and prescriptions, these approaches begin to address the interactions of classroom inhabitants. Classroom conflicts and the attempts at resolving those conflicts, be they positive communication or the establishment of a community, are actions and reactions that are connected to setting students up for success. These ideas open the doors to a new way of addressing behavior problems—student empowerment.

2

A New Perspective–
Empowering Students

To solve behavior problems in math class, we need to empower students! At the core, students need academic empowerment. Surrounding the core are learning empowerment, social empowerment, and emotional empowerment. This new perspective can be depicted as the empowerment triangle, strong enough to solve even the toughest behavior problems in math class. See Empowerment Triangle, Figure 2.1.

Figure 2.1   Empowerment Triangle

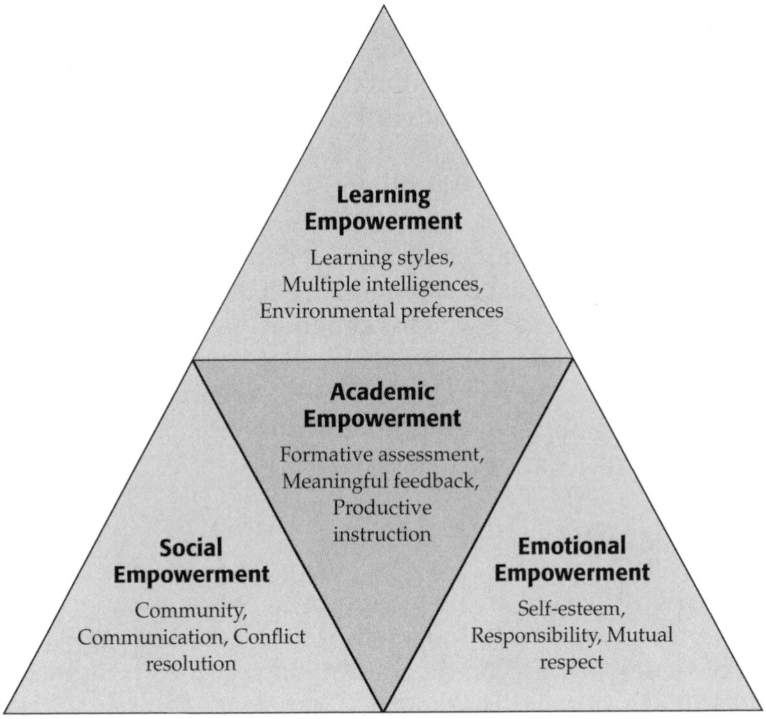

Learning Empowerment

Learning styles,
Multiple intelligences,
Environmental preferences

Academic Empowerment

Formative assessment,
Meaningful feedback,
Productive
instruction

Social Empowerment

Community,
Communication, Conflict
resolution

Emotional Empowerment

Self-esteem,
Responsibility, Mutual
respect

Academic Empowerment

Academic empowerment is the central component of solving behavior problems in math class. To academically empower students, teachers need to use formative assessments, meaningful feedback, and productive instruction.

Formative Assessments

Academic Empowerment involves using formative assessments to gather information about what a student knows and what the student needs to learn next. Many times the formative assessment serves as a preassessment that guides the instruction the teacher provides. When the instructional level is too high, the student may become frustrated. A frustrated student may resort to misbehavior to mask his inabilities to deal with the academic task. Similarly, if the instructional level is too low, the student may become bored. A bored student may resort to misbehavior simply to fill idle time. Using formative assessments to gather information about students' explicit academic needs serves to empower students (and the teacher!).

Meaningful Feedback

Meaningful feedback is another component of academic empowerment. Teachers need to engage in meaningful academic feedback with students to prompt students' thinking. Meaningful feedback is not giving answers; rather, it is guiding students and instructing them in ways that are beneficial. Meaningful feedback includes math discourse, guiding questions, appropriate prompts, academic coaching, and targeted teaching for students. The teacher encourages the students with needed support and challenge while offering the appropriate level of guidance and fostering student independence. Often meaningful feedback is provided in a one-to-one setting. Other times the teacher may offer meaningful feedback to individual students working in a group. Depending on the situation, meaningful feedback could be offered to several students who are working together on the same task. Meaningful feedback is very specific to the academic needs of individual students. It is an ongoing communication with students as they engage and move forward in the learning process.

Productive Instruction

Productive instruction, another component of academic empowerment, is often provided in a small group setting, but could be one-on-one. Productive instruction is based on the information gleaned from the student's responses to the formative assessment. The teacher's instruction is precise and catered to the student's exact and individual academic needs. The teacher adjusts the level of cognitive demand required by the student based on what the student needs at different times and with different tasks. Productive instruction often occurs in conjunction with meaningful feedback.

Learning Empowerment

Learning Empowerment involves students learning in the ways they learn best. Teachers need to help students by honoring learning styles, using multiple intelligences, and applying appropriate environmental preferences.

Learning Styles

Learning styles are different ways to learn. There are four main learning styles: visual, auditory, kinesthetic, and tactile (Dunn, Dunn, & Price, 1985). Visual learners learn best through seeing and reading. They prefer pictures, diagrams, charts, and graphic organizers. Auditory learners learn best through listening and speaking. They prefer discussion, stories, lectures, and songs. Kinesthetic learners learn best by doing and moving. They prefer physical activity. Tactile learners learn best by handling objects. They prefer hands-on learning with manipulatives and models. Some students have one dominant learning style. Other students have more than one style. The goal is to find out which learning style (or styles) best helps each student learn. Not only should the teacher know the students' learning styles, but students should know their own learning styles. Simple learning styles inventories can easily provide this information. Knowing and using their learning styles serve to provide students with learning empowerment. This is not to imply that students should always use their dominant learning style. It is important for students to experience a variety of approaches to learning. However, if a student is having difficulty, offering instruction that is catered to that student's precise learning style is more likely to empower the student and help the student find success.

Multiple Intelligences

Multiple-intelligences theory was first developed by Howard Gardner (1983, 1993, 1999). The theory started with seven intelligences; currently there are nine. These include music, word, picture, number, people, self, body, nature, and wondering. Everyone is made of certain amounts of each intelligence. Students may have stronger abilities in some intelligences than in other intelligences. Teachers should know their students' multiple intelligence profiles. Students as well should know their own multiple intelligence profiles.

Just as with the learning styles, there are plenty of multiple intelligences surveys available. It is a good idea to periodically retake the survey because multiple intelligence profiles can change. Knowing and using multiple intelligence information serve to provide students with learning empowerment. While students can benefit from a variety of approaches to learning, uncovering and using a student's multiple intelligence profile often offers the student a less complicated avenue toward success via learning empowerment.

Environmental Preferences

Environmental preferences include lighting, temperature, sound, spatial arrangement, and anything else related to the surroundings. Using environmental preferences information to enhance the student's learning styles can be productive (Dunn & Griggs, 2000). Some students prefer bright lights and some prefer soft lighting. Some students prefer warmth and others prefer chilly temperatures. Some students prefer background noise and others prefer quiet. Some students prefer open space and others prefer closer quarters. Teachers need to know and encourage the use of environmental preferences to give students learning empowerment. While some school buildings limit the teacher's ability to provide environmental preferences, it may be a simple change of desk location for a student that makes a positive difference.

Social Empowerment

Social Empowerment involves classroom community, communication, and conflict resolution. When these aspects are positive and productive, students are socially empowered.

Building a Positive Classroom Community

A positive classroom community is not established overnight. It takes time and work to develop a community, and it is an ongoing and ever-evolving process. There are a host of things to consider as we try to socially empower students by building a positive classroom community:

- The physical layout of the classroom invites collaboration.
- Students' opinions are valued and utilized.
- Support is authentic and available.
- Productive discourse and movement are encouraged.
- High expectations are owned by everyone.

- ◆ Everyone is respected.
- ◆ Students and teachers take responsibility seriously.
- ◆ Learning materials are available.
- ◆ Ground Rules are clear and fair.
- ◆ Humor (not sarcasm or misbehavior) is welcomed.
- ◆ Students and teachers are dedicated to learning.
- ◆ Everyone is included.
- ◆ Students and teachers work as a team (and participate in team-building exercises).
- ◆ Students and teachers give and receive respect.

Productive Communication

Productive communication is effectively giving and receiving information in ways that help, rather than hinder, teaching and learning. To enhance productive communication in the classroom, teachers need to model and require productive communication. There are some important things to remember as we help students become socially empowered through productive communication:

- ◆ Remember that how you say something is just as important as what you say!
- ◆ Model appropriate ways to express feelings, intentions, and expectations.
- ◆ Encourage and highlight student-to-student productive discourse.
- ◆ Clarify misinterpreted information and apologize if appropriate.
- ◆ Consider nonverbal communication.
- ◆ Use empowering words to express feelings, intentions, and expectations.

Conflict Resolution

Many conflict resolution models entail the three basic strategies of mediation, negotiation, and problem solving. Various models of conflict resolution encourage students to talk through their problem using specific steps and procedures. Some models include peers as mediators and the final judge being the teacher. In my experience, the best use of conflict resolution strategies involves solving problems and highlighting results, rather than following a set of scripted procedures. Students need to learn how to manage conflict as a means to help increase social empowerment for everyone.

Emotional Empowerment

Emotional Empowerment involves self-esteem, responsibility, and mutual respect. We want students to have high self-esteem, take responsibility, and engage in mutual respect with each other and with the teacher.

Self-esteem

Self-esteem involves how you see yourself and how you think others see you. One's perceived social status, self-worth, confidence, decision-making power, level of motivation, and degree of happiness play major roles in one's self-esteem. When thinking about the self-esteem of our students, we should consider these questions;

- ◆ Do my students think this class is worthwhile?

- ◆ Do my students think they are successful in our class?

- ◆ Do my students think I care about them?

- ◆ Do my students think I respect them?

- ◆ Are my students confident?

- ◆ Are my students motivated?

- ◆ Are my students happy?

Increasing our students' emotional empowerment involves increasing our students' self-esteem. But it is important that we do not attempt to do this in artificial ways. If we are looking over a chart of "100 ways to praise a student" to try to build self-esteem, we will most likely be unsuccessful because generic praise is not specific enough to have great impact. Students know the difference between real praise and fake praise. They also learn the difference between earned praise and unwarranted or haphazard praise. Specific, authentic encouragement is a more effective way to build a student's self-esteem.

Responsibility

Yelling at a student to "take responsibility" is not the way to help the student to actually take responsibility. Preaching about the need for students to take responsibility does not necessarily help them to do so either. We need to teach students how to take responsibility. As their teachers, we should model taking responsibility for our own actions. Teachers should take responsibility. Students should take responsibility. Everyone should understand that we are responsible for our own words, actions, and feelings.

We need to acknowledge and take ownership of our choices (both good and bad). We need to accept that blaming others does little to empower us. We need to move away from feeling sorry for ourselves because of what others have done. We need to focus on current and future choices so that we can be emotionally empowered.

Mutual Respect

Some teachers demand that students "show respect." But what they are really saying is "show submission." Respect does not have to be about submission. One can respect someone else without surrendering to that person. In some classrooms students are "required" to show respect to their teacher and classmates; yet many students do not know how to do so because their experiences with respect involve power and fear, rather than happiness and satisfaction. Showing respect is the best way to earn respect. We earn respect by acting in positive, productive, and responsible ways. To show respect to students, we should ask them how they feel, affirm their feelings, understand their feelings, show empathy, consider their perspectives, and make future decisions based on their thoughts, needs, and feelings. Mutual respect involves having positive feelings, words, and actions about and with one another. Maintaining mutual respect is an ongoing process that emotionally empowers students and teachers.

Ready for the Test?

Now that we have reviewed theories of blame, theories of remedy, and defined a new perspective for empowering students, let's look at fourteen different students and their math classes. Each scenario will be presented and then followed by a brief *True or False Quiz* that connects to the theories of blame. There will also be a *Multiple Choice Test* that connects to the theories of remedy (Note: The answer is always C). The solutions will then be offered in an *Essay Exam* format that will include possible strategies to increase the student's learning, social, or emotional empowerment in an attempt to repair the part of the student's empowerment triangle that is currently frail. The essays will also include ways to academically empower the students to further fortify their individual empowerment triangles and ways to help solve the behavior problems in each of the math classes (from kindergarten through twelfth grade).

Let's begin.

3

Kindergarten through Fifth Grade Math Students and Situations

The following chapter includes different math classroom situations and related solutions involving elementary school students. While these scenarios are presented in elementary settings, it is important to recognize that similar misbehaviors can occur with older students. Additionally, misbehaviors transcend gender, race, and culture. The scenarios presented are not intended to stereotype in any way. The goal is to look at specific misbehaviors and provide productive solutions.

Prepare to meet…Tonya Tantrum, Raymond the Runner, Screaming Scott, Booker the Bully, Lizbeth the Lifter, Disinterested Diondre, and Mouthy Maria.

Tonya Tantrum

Tonya is primary grade student who has temper tantrums when she does not get her way. Today during the math lesson, Tonya threw the pattern blocks across the table, fell on the floor, began screaming, and kicking her feet. Tonya's teacher tried to ignore this

behavior, but it was too distracting to the rest of the class. How could she teach when Tonya was making such a scene? So she yelled at Tonya to get her to stop screaming and kicking.

Problem Sources: True or False

1. This problem is Tonya's fault. She is a bad child. If she would just learn to behave, everything would be fine.

   False. Blaming Tonya and labeling her as a "bad" child does not help the situation. We need to find out why Tonya behaves in this manner and help her learn how to be a safe and responsible young student.

2. This problem is Tonya's parents' fault. They have not taught her how to behave in school.

   False. Blaming Tonya's parents for Tonya's behavior in school is simply a way to "pass the buck" so to speak. While Tonya's parents may benefit from some help with how to resolve Tonya's temper tantrums at home, the teacher needs to work with Tonya to resolve the temper tantrums in school.

3. Tonya has a behavior disorder. She needs medication to calm her down.

   False. Many young children have temper tantrums and very few of these children later manifest actual behavior disorders. Before jumping to medical solutions, we need to uncover the triggers for Tonya's misbehaviors and teach her some more appropriate responses.

4. The problem is that Tonya enjoys performing for the other children in the classroom. She likes the attention she receives when she displays this kind of behavior.

   False. Tonya is actually oblivious to her peers. The temper tantrum behavior is not intended to gather attention. Instead, it is the way Tonya responds to academic situations that are too difficult for her.

5. The problem is that Tonya's teacher does not know how to help Tonya behave appropriately.

   True. Screaming at someone to make her stop screaming is oxymoronic. Tonya needs role models of appropriate behavior. She also needs someone to teach her how to respond when she is frustrated.

6. The problem is that the pattern block activity is too difficult for Tonya. She does not have a strong foundation in spatial reasoning or visualization. Tonya is frustrated because she does not know how to place the pattern blocks in the correct locations on the template.

   True. To address these issues, Tonya needs academic empowerment and emotional empowerment.

Multiple Choice: Which Solution Will Work? A, B, or C

Solution A: Behavior modification with negative reinforcement

To solve this problem, Tonya's teacher needs to use negative reinforcement and simply ignore Tonya's temper tantrum. Tonya may only have the teacher's attention when she is behaving appropriately.

Why Solution A will not work for Tonya

Tonya's teacher has already tried to ignore Tonya's behavior. When this did not work, the teacher changed her tactics and yelled at Tonya. Brief inattention (ignoring) followed by intense attention (yelling) actually serves to positively reinforce the inappropriate behavior. Furthermore, throwing pattern blocks is dangerous. This behavior should not be ignored.

Solution B: Authoritarian rule with a time-out

To solve this problem, Tonya's teacher needs to take control of the situation and put Tonya in the "Time Out Chair."

Why Solution B will not work for Tonya

A little bit of history…The notion of "time out" derived from "time out from positive reinforcement" which was a practice developed many years ago to suppress certain behaviors in laboratory animals. Certainly, offering a little bit of space or time to get herself together to a child who is frustrated or otherwise annoyed can be an effective strategy (depending on the circumstances). Unfortunately, many teachers who employ time out use it as a punishment. If students are threatened with time out, it is a punishment. If students are humiliated by sitting in a "time out chair," it is a punishment. If students are afraid of time out, it is a punishment. Worse, some teachers have replaced the "Time Out Chair" with the "Thinking Chair." The child is supposed to think about what she has done. The major problem is that for the child who views the Thinking Chair as a punishment, we are teaching that child that *thinking is bad.* Not the message we want to send to our students.

Solution C: Academic empowerment and emotional empowerment

To solve this problem, Tonya's teacher needs to address Tonya's academic and emotional needs. The independent task assigned to Tonya (pattern blocks on a template) is too difficult. She is frustrated because she does not know how to do it. Tonya has learned that if she throws a temper tantrum she will not have to keep working on a task that she does not know how to do. The temper tantrum offers the results Tonya is seeking. Therefore, Tonya's teacher needs to address the academic needs by modifying the task and address Tonya's emotional needs by teaching her a more appropriate way to express her frustration.

Why Solution C will work for Tonya

If the independent task is situated at the right level, Tonya will be able to accomplish it without intense frustration. If the task needs to be at a higher level (to satisfy a standard or offer a challenge), Tonya's teacher should work with her individually or in a small group to offer some scaffolding so that Tonya can find success. To meet Tonya's emotional needs, the teacher needs to offer Tonya some appropriate ways to express frustration, better still, what to do before she becomes frustrated. These strategies will help Tonya strengthen her self-esteem and become more responsible.

Essay: Emotional Empowerment

Possible strategies

Tonya needs to know that she is allowed to ask for help when she does not know what to do. While we do not want Tonya to ask for help every minute, we do want her to begin recognizing oncoming frustration and seeking solutions. Tonya and the teacher can establish a signal that lets Tonya express her feelings and communicates the situation to the teacher. The signal could be a note card with a question mark on it that she is allowed to keep in her desk and post in a designated area when she needs the teacher's help. Tonya needs to understand that the teacher is not at Tonya's every beck and call, but that she will prioritize Tonya when she sees the question mark note card. If during the first couple of days, Tonya over uses the signal, the teacher and Tonya can meet to set a reasonable limit for how many times the signal can be used during the class time. This solution empowers Tonya within a manageable structure for the teacher.

Other strategies, such as asking a friend for help, may also be beneficial for Tonya. We want to teach Tonya to ask a question about the task, not simply announce, "I don't know what to do." Initially, the teacher may need to model some example questions that Tonya could ask. Asking task-related questions will help Tonya take charge of her learning.

To address the temper tantrums, Tonya and the teacher need to talk about appropriate ways to express frustration. It really is ok to be frustrated; it happens to all of us. We just need healthy avenues for expressing the frustration (not throwing things, falling on the floor, and kicking and screaming). Clay or play dough is sometimes helpful for children. They can squeeze it to release their frustration. Some children respond better if they are allowed to go get a drink of water or take a short walk when they feel frustrated. Tonya can try some of these releasers and Tonya and the teacher can evaluate the effectiveness and plan accordingly.

Responsibility

Using a signal to request help, asking a friend for help, and appropriately expressing frustration are ways that Tonya can be more responsible in the classroom. Tonya also needs to learn how to take responsibility for her choices even when they are not the right choices. Perhaps during the first week of implementing these strategies, Tonya slips back into her old way of dealing with frustration and starts a temper tantrum. The teacher can help Tonya by calmly reminding her of the strategies and allowing her time to gather her composure. If Tonya is able to do this without a full-blown tantrum or dangerous behavior, the teacher can encourage Tonya to take responsibility. The teacher may say, "Tonya, you stopped your temper tantrum very well. I am proud of you. Some of the blocks fell on the floor. Would you take care of that?" Picking up the blocks that fell during the brief tantrum provides Tonya with a way of taking responsibility. Ultimately, we would like for Tonya to apologize for her behavior as a way to take responsibility. However, making her "say sorry" is not an effective strategy. Tonya can learn to apologize by watching others do so. Responsibility is modeled for Tonya when the teacher takes responsibility and ownership of choices the teacher makes. The teacher may say, "Tonya, I am sorry that I yelled at you. I should have made a better choice." Apologizing to students when we make mistakes is very powerful.

Self-esteem

Sometimes teachers try to build a child's self-esteem by telling the child how wonderful she is and what a "good job" she is doing. These generic, nonspecific compliments are not especially helpful in building the child's self-esteem. However, highlighting specific positive behaviors is quite beneficial. "Tonya, it was a good idea to flip the block over and try to fit it in the template." "It was great how you stuck with the task even when it was hard for you." "Good job posting the question mark and waiting a few minutes until I could answer your question." These comments clearly denote the specific behaviors that the teacher wants to see Tonya continue to manifest. These comments also help Tonya learn how to take responsibility for her learning and her behavior because she knows specifically what she is doing right, which makes it easier for Tonya to continue to do these things!

Essay: Academic Empowerment

Formative assessment

To find out the source of Tonya's frustration and learn her misconceptions and gaps in knowledge associated with today's lesson, the teacher uses a high-quality, yet simple formative assessment.

Tonya's teacher modified the independent task Tonya was originally working on and used this as a formative assessment to gather information about Tonya's visualization and spatial reasoning skills.

The original task was too frustrating for Tonya. She did not know where to place the pattern blocks to complete the assignment.

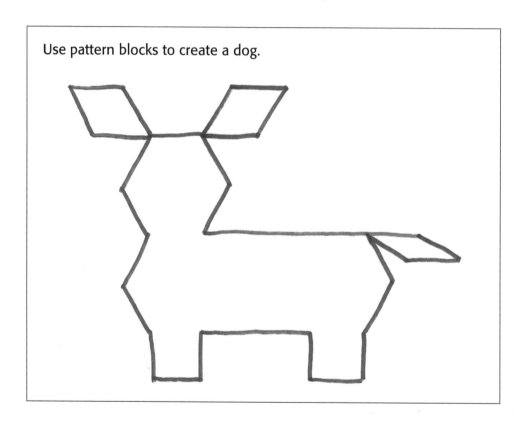

Use pattern blocks to create a dog.

The modified task allowed Tonya to complete the assignment. Using the lines and shading, she was able to place the pattern blocks in the correct locations. Tonya was engaged in the task without frustration.

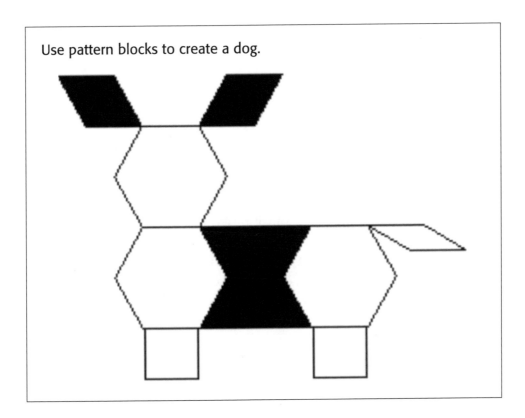

Use pattern blocks to create a dog.

Using both the original task and the modified task as formative assessments, the teacher now knows the appropriate instructional level for Tonya. The modified task is appropriate for Tonya to work on independently. The original task needs more direct instruction from the teacher.

Meaningful feedback

Tonya's teacher works with Tonya and a few other students who are working at a similar level. The teacher wants to help the students learn more about the relationships between and among the pattern block shapes to help increase the students' visualization and spatial reasoning abilities.

> **Teacher**   Let's explore with the pattern blocks to find out how they are related.
>
> **Tonya**   What do you mean?

Teacher	Look at the yellow hexagon (focuses on the face of the hexagonal prism). Which blocks could be used to make the same shape?
	The students investigate the pattern blocks, but no one offers a verbal response.
Teacher	What if you stack some red trapezoid blocks on top of the yellow hexagon block?
	The students try the task and discover that it takes two trapezoid blocks to equal the size of the yellow hexagon block.
Teacher	What about the other blocks?
	Prompted by the question, the students try stacking other blocks on the yellow hexagon block. They find that three blue rhombus blocks or six green triangle blocks are equal in size to the yellow hexagon block.
Teacher	So how can we use this information when you are working with one of the templates?
Tonya	You can decide how you want to fill it up.
Teacher	Tell us more about what you mean.
Tonya	You could use a yellow one, two red ones, or three blue ones.
Another student	Or six green triangles.
	The students agree.

The feedback offered by the teacher in this mini-lesson is very meaningful. Guided by the questions Tonya and the other students learn about the relationships between and among some of the pattern blocks. They use a hands-on approach to verify their answers by proving their answers with pattern block models. The teacher's invitation to "tell more" offers a way for Tonya to further explain her math thinking. The meaningful and individualized feedback provided in this mini-lesson builds foundations for the students that will help them as they work with more complex pattern block templates.

Productive instruction

Using a different template (without lines or shading), Tonya's teacher works with a small group of students to teach them how to use different pattern blocks to fill the same templates. Each student has a template and some pattern blocks. They are asked to fill the template design in different ways. After each student is finished, they compare the different ways each one filled the template. Some of the students' comments include, "I used four yellow hexagons, but you used eight red trapezoids." I tried to use as many green triangles as I could. I have a lot." Tonya announced, "Everyone is different, but everyone is right!"

Final thoughts

The next day, Tonya's teacher allowed Tonya to choose which type of pattern block template she wanted to work with during independent practice…a template with lines and shading or a template without lines and shading. This choice helps Tonya take responsibility, serving to empower Tonya emotionally and academically. Interestingly, Tonya chose the template without lines and shading because she wanted to try "the tricky one." Because she was empowered, she was ready for the challenge.

Raymond the Runner

Raymond is a flight risk. At any given time, he may run out of the classroom door and out of the school. Today, the students were involved in a ten-frame flash game. Students were working in pairs to briefly show a ten frame with a certain number of dots on it while the partner named the quantity of dots. Raymond did not want to name the number of dots. Instead, he only wanted to show the card to his partner. His partner grabbed the ten frame cards and demanded that they "take turns." Raymond flew out of his chair and out of the door. Raymond's teacher ran out of the classroom calling "Raymond, come back here!"

Problem Sources: True or False

1. This problem is Raymond's fault. He is too immature to be in this class.

   False. Blaming Raymond's immaturity serves as an excuse. Implying that Raymond is not ready for his current class feeds the problem rather than working toward fixing the problem.

2. This problem is Raymond's mother's fault. Raymond runs away from her all the time. She never does anything to punish him. So he just keeps running away.

   False. While Raymond's mother may need some assistance to help her stop Raymond from running away from her, the teacher and Raymond need to work on Raymond's in-school running episodes.

3. The problem is that Raymond has RD (running disorder). He needs medication to make him stay in the classroom.

   False. There is no such thing as "running disorder."

4. The problem is that Raymond wants to perform for his classmates. He loves the attention of everyone yelling for him to come back.

   False. Raymond is not running to entertain his classmates. In fact, Raymond runs so often that the other students barely take notice.

5. The problem is that the teacher does not know what to do when Raymond runs.

   True. The teacher should not leave the classroom (unless there is adequate adult supervision). The teacher and other key educators in the building need a strategic plan for when Raymond runs.

6. The problem is that Raymond does not know how to "subitize" quantities (recognize quantities without counting) on the ten frame and Raymond has difficulties dealing with conflict.

   True. To address these issues, Raymond needs academic empowerment and social empowerment.

———————◆———————

Multiple Choice: Which Solution Will Work? A, B, or C

Solution A: Behavior modification with a positive reinforcement

To solve this problem, Raymond should have a sticker chart. For every hour that Raymond stays in the classroom he will earn a special "goofy monster" sticker.

Why Solution A will not work for Raymond

Raymond does not have any particular interest in stickers. Typical stickers are not appealing to him. Thus, the reward does not serve to reward him. Worse, these "goofy monster" stickers actually evoke fear in Raymond because he often has nightmares about monsters. Therefore, the reward is actually serving as a punishment for the desired behavior. Yikes!

Solution B: Authoritarian rule with a fear tactic

To solve this problem, the teacher needs to signal the office when Raymond runs so that an alarm can sound. Upon hearing the alarm, all available educators run down the halls looking for Raymond. If Raymond approaches a door, the educator is directed to yell "Stop Raymond!" and physically restrain him.

Why Solution B will not work for Raymond

The alarm scares Raymond, which makes him run faster. "All available educators running down the hall" is not a strategic plan. It is chaotic and disorganized. Moreover, when someone yells at Raymond, he runs in the opposite direction. Fear is one of the sources of Raymond's inappropriate behavior, so using fear as a solution is counterproductive. For safety and legal reasons, the physical restraint of a student should not be done by one educator and its use should be minimized.

Solution C: Academic empowerment and social empowerment

To solve this problem, Raymond's teacher needs to address his academic needs and his social needs. Because Raymond does not know how to subitize quantities on the ten frame, he is not finding success or satisfaction with the partner activity. He needs a stronger foundation in number sense. Furthermore, Raymond is afraid of conflict. So when the other student grabbed the ten frames and demanded that they take turns, Raymond chose flight over fight and took off running.

Why Solution C will work for Raymond

If the teacher works with Raymond to strengthen his number sense via more experiences with subitizing, he will be able to find success when working with a partner. Raymond's social needs can be met by teaching him more appropriate responses to potential conflict.

Essay: Social Empowerment

Possible strategies

Raymond needs to understand how to deal with potential conflict. One strategy for doing so is for him to clearly state his feeling. "I am scared when you yell" is a simple, yet profound statement that Raymond can use to let others know how he is feeling. Raymond may need some role playing or modeling for him to gain comfort with clearly expressing his feelings. For example, the teacher may use puppets or other imaginary characters to portray effective ways of stating feelings during confrontational situations.

Another strategy that the teacher can use is to set up boundaries for Raymond. He needs a place to go when his "flight" response surfaces. A place in the classroom can be designated as Raymond's safety zone. This safety zone could be as simple as a pillow beside the teacher's desk or it may be a more elaborate set-up. The point is that Raymond feels safe in this place and can easily go there when he feels he needs to do so. Raymond and the teacher can evaluate the usage and effectiveness of the safety zone by analyzing how often he goes to the safety zone, how long he stays there, and if periodically going to the safety zone is beneficial for him. The long-term goal is for Raymond to use the safety zone less and less.

If running out of the classroom persists, the teacher can establish a signal that alerts designated school personnel when Raymond leaves the classroom. Rather than a loud alarm, the signal could be a calm code call to the office such as, "Room 3 requests assistance." Office personnel know this code and contact the Crisis Team (for example, principal, assistant principal, counselor, and nonclassroom teacher). One member of the Crisis Team goes to the classroom to cover for the teacher; the others stand in the hallways at specific locations. No running. No screaming. No chaos. Everyone remains calm. With this plan, Raymond is less likely to panic and more likely to be able to go back to his classroom in a safe, calm, and more timely manner.

Conflict resolution

It may help to establish a conflict resolution plan in Raymond's classroom. Communication is the key component in the initial stages of conflict resolution. Students are encouraged to calmly express feelings as they negotiate to reach a productive agreement. If needed, the students can go to a designated peer or the teacher to help them come to an agreement.

Essay: Academic Empowerment

Formative assessment

To find out the academic source of Raymond's misbehavior in class today, the teacher uses a high-quality yet simple formative assessment.

The teacher works with Raymond to find out if he can subitize by rolling a die and asking how many dots are showing. The teacher analyzes how quickly and accurately Raymond responds. Counting takes time. Subitizing is instant. Raymond is able to subitize all of the quantities on a standard die. To determine if Raymond can subitize quantities on the ten frame, she flashes several cards (one at a time) and asks how many. Raymond counts the dots on each card. He does not subitize the quantities. The teacher has found the level at which Raymond encounters difficulty and can use this information to plan for Raymond's meaningful feedback and productive instruction. (This formative assessment appears in *Math intervention: Building number power with formative assessment, differentiation, and games. Grades PreK-2* by J. Taylor-Cox, 2009, Larchmont, NY: Eye on Education. Copyright 2009 by Eye on Education. Reprinted with permission.)

Meaningful feedback

The teacher works with a small group of students including Raymond. She shows the students a ten frame with one dot on it and asks, "How many dots?"

Students	One.
Teacher	Raymond, how do you know it is one?
Raymond	It is easy. It is just one.
Teacher	So what will two look like?
Students	Just one more.
Teacher	What about three?
Raymond	Another one.
Teacher	What about these? *(the teacher shows the four and five ten frames)*
Student	That's four and that's five.
Teacher	How would you describe the five?
Raymond	The whole row is full.
Students	But not the bottom row.
Teacher	What if the whole frame was full?

The students think about this and the teacher displays the full ten frame.

Student	It has to be ten.
Teacher	How do you know?
Raymond	It is all filled up.
Teacher	What if there was one less?
Student	It would be nine.
Teacher	How could you describe the nine?
Raymond	It is missing one. That's all.
Teacher	What if two were missing?
Raymond	Eight.
Teacher	Wow, Raymond. How did you figure that out?
Raymond	Eight comes before nine.
	The other students agree.

This meaningful feedback continues as the students engage in further math discourse involving the other quantities on the ten frame. Raymond's final comment is "I get it now. You just have to use what you know to figure out what you don't know." That's a nice way to describe the process of subitizing, Raymond!

The feedback offered in this mini-lesson is very powerful. The teacher helps Raymond use what he knows to figure out what he does not yet know when subitizing on the ten frame. This helps build Raymond's foundations in number sense and his self-esteem.

Productive instruction

After the feedback, Raymond and the other students in his group are ready to try the ten frame flash activity. Because his foundation in number sense is stronger and he has positive experiences with subitizing quantities on the ten frame, Raymond is able to successfully participate. The teacher meets with the group the following day to introduce subitizing eleven and twelve using two ten frames. Each student has a ten frame and counters. The teacher asks the students to "show ten." Each student fills his ten frame accurately and the teacher asks the students to describe the quantity. Afterwards, the teacher poses this question, "What if I gave you one more counter? Raymond answers, "It would not fit." The other students agree. The teacher continues the activity by sharing that they could each have another ten frame. The students decide that it would be eleven because "eleven is one more than ten." Each student uses two ten frames to show eleven. The teacher asks the students to show twelve and discuss how twelve looks and how they know it is twelve with their partners. Because the students are having great success, the teacher decides to introduce thirteen, fourteen, and fifteen. At the conclusion of the mini-lesson, the students express confidence in subitizing quantities of ten and up to five more using two ten frames. Raymond announces, "I think I might be ready for even more, soon!"

Final thoughts

Over the next week, Raymond chose to play the ten-frame flash game several times during "choice time." He even initiated playing the game with two ten frames (full ten plus various other quantities). Although he used the safety zone several times during the first week, his use of the designated area began to subside after that because he continued to be socially and academically empowered.

Screaming Scott

Several times a day Scott goes into a screaming fit. His screams are so loud that the other students cannot concentrate. Today, Scott was fine during the whole group portion of the lesson on patterns; however, when the teacher asked the students to move into small groups, Scott fell to his knees and began screaming at the top of his lungs. The teacher rolled her eyes and yelled at Scott, "Try to be as loud as you can. We love it when you scream!" Then she called the main office, announcing through the intercom, "Scott is at it again! Please send someone to remove him. And send some ear plugs for me!"

Problem Sources: True or False

1. This problem is Scott's fault. If he would just stop screaming, he would be normal.

   False. Scott is not abnormal because he screams.

2. This problem is Scott's parents' fault. They let him scream whenever and wherever he wants.

   False. Blaming Scott's parents does not help resolve Scott's classroom misbehavior.

3. The problem is that Scott has a hearing problem and therefore does not know how loud his screams actually are.

   False. Scott's pediatrician has tested Scott's hearing and found that Scott does not have a hearing problem.

4. The problem is that Scott does not have any friends. If he had some friends, he would stop screaming.

   False. While Scott may benefit from positive peer relationships, his screaming problem has little to do with his peers.

5. The problem is that Scott's teacher uses sarcasm and models inappropriate behavior.

   True. When the teacher yells at Scott, she is modeling the exact behavior that she does not want in the classroom. It is paradoxical to scream at someone to make that person stop screaming. Furthermore, the sarcasm the teacher uses serves to belittle Scott and thereby teaches the other students that demeaning others with sarcasm is acceptable, even encouraged, in this classroom.

6. The problem is that Scott has difficulties transitioning from one group structure to the next. The problem becomes more profound when Scott is not feeling confident about the content.

   True. To address these issues, Scott needs learning empowerment and academic empowerment.

Multiple Choice: Which Solution Will Work? A, B, or C

Solution A: Behavior modification with a reward

To solve this problem, Scott will earn free play time if he makes it through the day without screaming. For Scott, "a scream-free day equals play."

Why Solution A will not work for Scott

Currently, Scott has screaming episodes several times a day. Having an entire day without screaming is a goal that needs to be incrementally achieved. It may be beneficial for Scott to receive a reward at scream-free hour increments. As Scott finds success, the teacher could move to scream-free mornings and scream-free afternoons. Knowing that the reward only serves to teach temporary compliance, the teacher needs to wean Scott from the reward as he finds success. By focusing on Scott's successes, the teacher can help Scott want to have a scream-free day whether he is rewarded with "play" or not.

Solution B: Behavior modification with a punishment

To solve this problem, we need to incorporate a punishment for Scott. Every time he goes into a screaming fit, he needs to be sent to the office, and a phone call home needs to be made.

Why Solution B will not work for Scott

Calling home to report Scott's screaming fits will not work because Scott's parents do not know how to solve Scott's screaming episodes. In fact, Scott's screaming is even more frequent at home than it is at school. We need to uncover why Scott is screaming to help him stop screaming.

Solution C: Academic empowerment and learning empowerment

To solve this problem, Scott's teacher needs to address his academic needs and his learning needs. Scott's learning environment is not working for him because he struggles with transitions. When the group structure changes, when the students move to a different location, or when any other transition occurs, Scott is distressed. He has learned to cope by screaming his way through it. We need to teach Scott more appropriate ways to deal with transitions, modify his learning environment, and academically empower Scott so that he can be successful.

Why Solution C will work for Scott

Uncovering why Scott has such adverse responses to transitions is an important initial step. Creating an environment that helps Scott transition more smoothly and adjusting the initial level of cognitive demand required at the onset of the transition will give Scott academic and learning empowerment.

———————◆———————

Essay: Learning Empowerment

Possible strategies

After a meeting with Scott's parents and the school counselor, Scott's teacher learned that Scott was involved in a fatal car accident that left him as the only survivor. His aunt and sister died, as well as the other driver. Scott was trapped in the car for several hours before being rescued by paramedics. He spent two months recovering in the hospital. Scott's therapist believes Scott is still suffering from post-traumatic stress syndrome. Fear of transition is connected to the fear associated with the traumatic event. Uncovering this information helped the teacher make sense of what is happening in the classroom.

To help Scott ease into each new transition, Scott's teacher invited Scott to bring something from home that represents comfort and happiness. With the help of his parents, Scott selected a special cartoon hand towel that was given to him on his birthday. Scott will hold the small towel during the school day to remind him that the classroom is a safe and happy place.

Another strategy that the teacher can try is to give Scott a more appropriate way to express his fear by replacing the screaming with a soft instrument. Scott's teacher borrowed a small xylophone from the music teacher for Scott to use. The teacher and Scott will play the xylophone together to "announce" approaching transitions to the class. This new routine gives Scott notice that the transition is coming and distracts his fear with an important task (announcing the transition with the xylophone). The sound of the instrument replaces the sound of screaming allowing Scott to focus on learning.

Environmental preferences

During mathematics the students work at four different math centers (including the teacher-led small group as one of the centers). To help Scott be successful, the teacher can develop a simple timeline with Scott so that he is aware of all the transitions prior to the actual transitions. The teacher took photographs of each center (and one of herself) to use in Scott's timeline. Together they added the times that Scott would start each new center. This timeline served as a way for Scott to anticipate and manage transitions (and he learned to tell time by the quarter hour!).

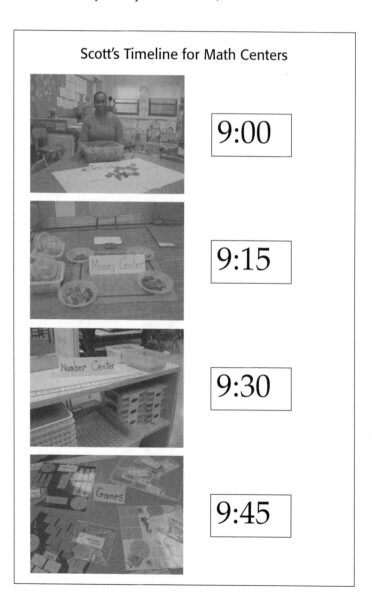

Scott's Timeline for Math Centers

To further connect with Scott's environmental preferences, the physical layout of the classroom needed to be adjusted. The teacher realized that Scott transitioned best when he could actually see the next location prior to the time of transition. In some ways viewing the next location helped Scott prepare for the transition. Rearranging the tables gave Scott (and the other students) the ability to view all of the stations. Additionally, the teacher moved Scott's desk to the center of the classroom to give him a better connection to all of the locations around him. This, too, helped improve Scott's ability to transition.

Essay: Academic Empowerment

Formative assessment

To find out how to academically empower Scott, the teacher uses a high-quality yet simple formative assessment.

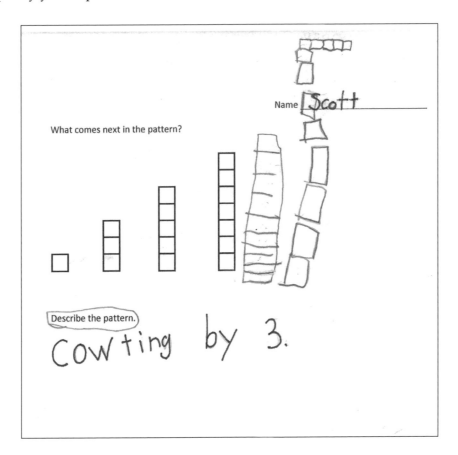

During this unit on algebraic thinking, the students have worked with repeating patterns and are now beginning to learn about growing patterns. The formative assessment includes a pattern that the students have not yet worked with because the teacher wants to preassess the students to find out how to cater the instruction. Even though Scott's responses are inaccurate, they do reveal that he has some understanding of growing patterns that "cowt" by a constant amount. Scott is not working at a low level or at a high level with growing patterns. He is working in an "on-grade-level" range and is ready for instruction. However, the teacher has noticed that Scott is often not at his best when he begins a new task. He often makes an error (e.g., miscounting) when faced with something new to him. Yet, if there are two tasks and the first one is something familiar to Scott, he seems to do better on the second (unfamiliar) task. Therefore the teacher incorporates this adjustment in the level of cognitive demand required by Scott for the initial task. In essence, Scott will have a task that he can easily do first, followed by a task that might be new or otherwise challenging.

Meaningful feedback

The teacher gives Scott some connecting cubes and asks him to create towers that increase in size by one cube.

Scott	Do you mean like the patterns that we did yesterday?
Teacher	Yes. How would you describe those patterns?
Scott	They were nice.
Teacher	Yes. They were nice. How would you describe the patterns with math words?
Scott	They were "grow by one" patterns.
Teacher	Yes. I see you have made another "grow by one" pattern here.
Scott	Yep. Right here.
Teacher	What do you think a "grow by two" pattern would look like?
Scott	I don't know. I guess it gets bigger by two.
Teacher	Exactly. Use the cubes to show a "grow by two" pattern.
	The teacher leaves Scott for awhile to go work with other students. When she returns, Scott has not only created a +2 pattern, but he has also used different colored cubes to make a +3 pattern.
Teacher	Wow, Scott. Tell me about what you have here.
Scott	This is a "grow by two pattern." Then I thought, if it can "grow by two" it can "grow by three." So I made it like that.

Teacher	Great thinking! Do you think there are other growing patterns?
Scott	Yep. I think growing patterns can grow by anything! If you know it, you can show it.
Teacher	That's an awesome way to describe it!

The feedback offered by the teacher helps Scott move to the next level in his thinking about growing patterns. Because Scott was given the right amount of guidance, support, and challenge he was able to make great progress.

Productive instruction

The teacher works with Scott and some other students in a small group setting. After the students create a "grow by five" pattern with cubes, the teacher asks the students to think about other names for this pattern. "The getting bigger by five pattern," says one students. "We could say the plus five pattern" adds another student. The other students agree.

Then the teacher asks the students to think about how they could record this +5 pattern. The students discuss drawing pictures. Scott asks, "It would be really easy if we could just write the numbers." The others agree. Encouraged by the teacher, the students record the "grow by five pattern" in this way; 5101520253035. "That doesn't look right!" says one of the students, "We need some spaces." The teacher suggests that they separate the terms using commas. The students quickly implement the idea. Using mini-dry-erase boards and markers the students create different growing patterns with numbers. They share the patterns with each other and try to name the next terms.

Final thoughts

Over the next few months, Scott's screaming episodes declined to a bare minimum. It was only sudden transitions (e.g., fire drills) that caused Scott to scream and even those severe transitions were tempered when the teacher began to encourage Scott to carry and play the xylophone as the class exited the building. Analyzing the situation and allowing the environmental changes proved productive for Scott. His math ability began to flourish as the teacher continued to use the strategy of providing tasks that require a lower level of cognitive demand before moving to tasks that require a higher level of cognitive demand.

Booker the Bully

Booker verbally threatens and taunts other students. He constantly says, "I'm gonna get you!" or "You're dead meat!" to his classmates. If he sees a math game he wants to play or finds a place where he wants to sit, he just tells the students who are already there to "Go away!" If someone has something he wants, he  just takes it. Furthermore, Booker enjoys the scene when he releases gas. It is almost as if he can do this on command. He sits down, lets one rip, and then enjoys the reaction from all those around him. Today, when it was time for the whole class to gather together, he came to the group, told one student to move, then sat down and farted. He laughed loudly when those around him reacted. Some shrieked, "Eeeew!" Others chuckled and nearly applauded. Frustrated with Booker's disruptions and threats, the teacher screamed, "Get your smelly self out of my class and to the office." Booker laughed and walked out.

Problem Solutions: True or False

1. This problem is that Booker is mean and disgusting.

   False. Booker may act mean and have some vulgar habits, but calling him mean and disgusting does not help the situation.

2. This problem is Booker's father. He is mean to Booker and Booker takes it out on his peers.

   Maybe True. It is common that bullies have a history of being bullied, but blaming Booker's father does not solve the problem.

3. The problem is that Booker has Conduct Disorder. He is intimidating, aggressive, and a constant behavior problem.

   False. Although Conduct Disorder is a recognized disorder, Booker does not have it.

4. The problem is Booker's peers let him bully them. They need to stop acting like victims.

   False. Blaming victims and telling them to stop being victims is not an effective way to solve the problem.

5. The problem is that Booker's teacher lets him get away with misbehaving for a time and then explodes with anger.

   True. Allowing Booker to bully students is not acceptable. Exploding with anger, name calling, and kicking him out of class are ways that the teacher is actually bullying Booker.

6. The problem is that the work is actually too easy for Booker. He's bored and has too much idle time. He needs to be academically challenged and his emotional issues need to be addressed.

   True. To address these issues, Booker needs academic empowerment and emotional empowerment.

Multiple Choice: Which Solution Will Work? A, B, or C

Solution A: Behavior modification with behavior grades

To solve this problem, the teacher needs to put Booker on a behavior modification plan that includes nonacademic behavior grades. For every math class period that Booker completely refrains from bullying and passing gas, he will receive the letter grade A. If he is close to completely refraining from the misbehaviors, he will receive the letter grade B. If he partially refrains, he will receive the letter grade C. The letter grade D will be received if he only refrains slightly and letter grade F will be received if he completely fails to refrain from these misbehaviors. At the end of the week, the teacher will average the behavior grades.

Why Solution A will not work for Booker

Behavior grades will not offer any incentive for Booker. He already knows that he behaves poorly. He does not need behavior grades to prove this. Furthermore, there is great degree of teacher subjectivity built into this behavior modification plan. What is the actual difference between grade C and grade D behavior? Do we want to send the message that superlative behavior (grade A) is equivalent to refraining from misbehavior? Another major problem with this plan is that young children do not truly understand how to earn grades. They often think grades (behavior or academic) are simply a reflection of how much the teacher likes or dislikes them.

Solution B: Authoritarian rule with a punishment

To solve this problem, Booker will pay for his offenses with recess time. Every time he bullies someone or passes gas, he will lose ten minutes of recess. If he has a really bad day, he will go into recess time debt. If he has a good day, he will get to have recess.

Why Solution B will not work for Booker

Booker already misses recess on a regular basis. The punishment is not serving as a deterrent and is therefore ineffective. Furthermore, Booker is very active and needs recess time to release some of his energy (and gas!).

Solution C: Academic empowerment & emotional empowerment

To solve this problem, Booker needs to be challenged academically with tasks and lessons that are aimed at his level. He also needs help with his self-esteem and with taking responsibility.

Why Solution C will work for Booker

Instruction geared toward his level will academically empower Booker. Learning how to take responsibility and improving his self-esteem will emotionally empower Booker.

Essay: Emotional Empowerment

Possible strategies

The bullying must stop. No one should have to endure threats, taunts, or harassment. We need an environment that is safe so that the students can focus on learning math. There should be school-wide definitions and consequences for bullying so that everyone is aware of what bullying is and what will happen if someone acts like a bully. Teachers should never ignore bullying because that sends the message that it is acceptable. When bullying occurs, stop it immediately by following some simple steps. (1) Label it. "This is bullying!" (2) State that it is unacceptable. "Bullying is not allowed in our school." (3) Remind the bully of the established consequence. "If someone acts like a bully, he must go to the office." (4) Enforce the consequence. (5) Debrief separately with everyone involved (bully, victim, and bystanders) to help them learn how to stop bullying.

Self-esteem

Most bullies have low self-esteem. They use bullying to assert dominance in order to compensate for their insecurities. Many have been bullied in the past and know what it feels like to be the victim. We need to help the bully find other ways to increase his self-esteem. Highlighting what the student does well and directing his attention to appropriate ways of communicating his plans and desires will help increase his self-esteem and inter-relationship skills.

Many victims of bullying also have personal insecurities. It is important not to embarrass the victim further when stopping a bullying situation. Don't say, "Why did you let him do that?" or "Stand up for yourself!" These comments do not serve to empower the victim; instead these comments make the victim feel worse. It is better to talk to the victim after the situation and in private. Teachers need to help victims learn successful strategies when faced with a bully. The victim can use humor to deflect the bully's comments. The victim can ignore the bully and walk away. The victim can state the facts, "Bullying is not allowed. I choose to walk away." The victim needs a safe way to report the bullying so that it will be stopped and ultimately prevented.

Responsibility

Following through with the consequence for the bully is an important way for the bully to learn to accept responsibility for his actions. He needs to claim his actions so that he can be empowered to change his actions. Responsibility involves taking ownership of the things we do, good or bad. Our actions are not caused by others. We have the power to react in the way that we choose, regardless of what someone else does or says.

The Bully-Free Zone

Creating a Bully-Free Zone in the classroom involves everyone. The students need to talk about what bullying is and how it disrupts the learning environment. Everyone needs to work together to establish a classroom culture where people care about one another. The students and teacher may want to sign a class contract giving support and commitment to the Bully-Free concept. It is even better if the entire school is involved in developing a schoolwide bully-free zone. The idea also gives the students an easier way to stop bullying. If someone is bullying, the victim or a bystander can give a reminder by saying, "Our classroom (or our school) is a bully-free zone."

Solving the gas problem

First, we need to find out if Booker has a health issue that is causing this problem. The teacher should ask Booker and, if necessary, seek consultation with the school nurse and Booker's parents. The issue should be presented as factual as possible and out of concern for Booker.

Another option is for the teacher to use an automatic air freshener strategically placed in the group time area. Further options include empowering Booker to excuse himself from class to go to the restroom when necessary. Of course, this strategy (and all other strategies) needs to be evaluated for effectiveness. Is the strategy working or do we need to try a different strategy?

Essay: Academic Empowerment

Formative assessment

To find out how to academically empower Booker, the teacher uses a simple, yet informative assessment. The class is getting ready to begin a unit on subtraction with two-digit numbers. The teacher uses this formative assessment to preassess Booker.

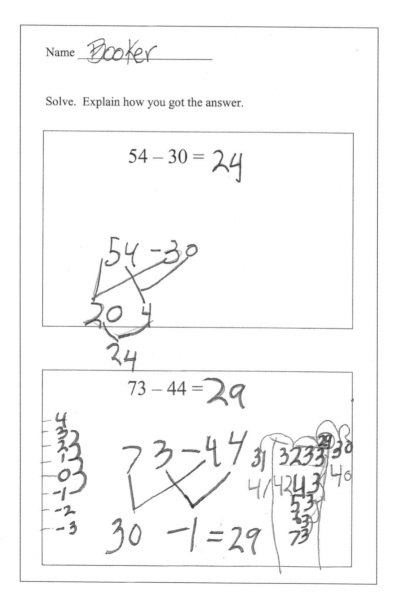

Booker's answers and explanations are quite advanced. He uses the partial differences strategy to solve both problems. He indicates that $50 - 30 = 20$ and $4 - 0 = 4$ and then combines the differences; $20 + 4 = 24$. He uses the same strategy when working with the regrouping situation, $70 - 40 = 30$ and $3 - 4 = -1$ and then combines the differences; $30 - 1 = 29$. He provides evidence that $3 - 4 = -1$ using a vertical number line. Furthermore, Booker shows how the answer can be obtained using a chunk of the hundred chart; $73 - 10 = 63$, $63 - 10 = 53$, $53 - 10 = 43$, $43 - 10 = 33$; $33 - 1 = 32$, $32 - 1 = 31$, $31 - 1 = 30$, and $30 - 1 = 29$. It is very obvious that Booker understands the content. He already knows how to subtract with and without regrouping. He will be bored unless the teacher provides an appropriate challenge.

Meaningful feedback

The teacher presents subtraction with three-digit numbers within a problem solving context to Booker.

Teacher	If you have $839 and I have $564, how would you figure out how much more money you have than I have?
Booker	I'm not sure. You wouldn't add them, so I guess you would subtract.
Teacher	Yes. This is a comparison subtraction situation.
Booker	Eight-hundred minus five hundred equals three-hundred.
Teacher	Great start.
Booker	Thirty-nine minus sixty-four. I am going to need a big number line.
Teacher	Tell me what you would do with a large number line.
Booker	I would start on 39 and subtract by making 64 jumps.
Teacher	Yes. That would work. Another way to do it is to think about 839 as 7 hundreds and 13 tens and 9 ones.
Booker	Why?
Teacher	Decomposing 839 into $700 + 130 + 9$ allows you to subtract more quickly.
Booker	Oh, I get it. You just subtract 60 from 130, which leaves 70. Then you subtract 4 from 9.
Teacher	Yes. So how much more money do you have than I have?

Booker writes, $700 - 500 = \boxed{200}$ $130 - 60 = \boxed{70}$ $9 - 4 = \boxed{5}$ $\boxed{275}$

Booker	It is $275!

Teacher	You have it! Try comparing two other dollar amounts, but this time we want to use dollars and change!
Booker	I can make up the amounts?
Teacher	Yes. Give it a try. I'll be back to see what you've done.

The feedback offered to Booker in this brief exchange is very powerful. Booker is given a more challenging problem and taught how to use the partial differences in another way. His understanding of how to use the number line to solve subtraction with regrouping problems is very strong. It was a strategic move on the teacher's part to give him a problem that would be cumbersome to solve on the number line. This opened the door for the teacher to teach Booker how to decompose the minuend to make it easier to subtract from it. The new strategy helps Booker increase his efficiency and mental math abilities. The teacher increases the level of cognitive demand required from Booker when she gives him a challenging, open-ended problem to work on by himself.

Productive instruction

The teacher worked with a small group of students, including Booker. The students worked with partners to play a game involving the partial differences strategy. The students flipped number cards to create subtraction expressions and called out the partial differences. Even though this game was not academically challenging for Booker (because of his advanced level), it provided a vehicle for empowering Booker emotionally. During this game, Booker used his intellect rather than bullying. He helped his partner gain knowledge of the content. The teacher complimented Booker's positive interactions with his partner. His partner even thanked Booker for "teaching" him how to play the game. Booker excused himself at one point during the game to go to the restroom. A look of relief on the students' faces was apparent. Later, the teacher showed Booker how he can play the same game using larger quantities, which provided academic content that was aimed at his level.

Final thoughts

Booker's bullying subsided over the next several weeks. During a class meeting the students shared how much they liked the new "Bully-Free Zone" that they had created in the classroom. One student (who had been bullied in the past) went over to shake Booker's hand. The rest of the class cheered. Not only did the classroom become a Bully-Free Zone, it also became an "Odor-Free Zone" because Booker learned to take responsibility for his actions.

Lizbeth the Lifter

Goldfish		4
Hamster		10
Snake		2
Turtle		7

The teacher suspects that Lizbeth has taken things that are not hers. Things often come up missing when Lizbeth is on the scene. Today the students were working with partners to collect, organize, and analyze data. During the assignment, Lizbeth disappeared into the area where all the backpacks are kept. Later, one of the students came to the teacher crying about the missing keychain that was once on her backpack. The teacher called out, "Lizbeth, empty your pockets!" Lizbeth looked sheepishly at the teacher and emptied her pockets. The keychain was not there. "Where is it?" asked the teacher. Lizbeth responded, "I don't know. Maybe we should look for it." The frustrated teacher said, "You are going to look for it today after school!"

Problem Sources: True or False

1. This problem is that Lizbeth is a juvenile delinquent.

   False. Lizbeth is not a juvenile delinquent.

2. This problem is that Lizbeth's parents do not punish her when she is accused of stealing.

   False. Just because Lizbeth is accused of stealing does not mean she is guilty of stealing. Therefore, voicing concerns about Lizbeth's parents or punishing her is not the right thing to do.

3. Lizbeth has kleptomania. She cannot control her urge to take things.

   False. Lizbeth is not a kleptomaniac.

4. The problem is Lizbeth does not like her classmates, so she wants to take things from them.

   False. Lizbeth does like her classmates. She wants to get along with them.

5. The problem is that Lizbeth's teacher accuses Lizbeth of stealing without concrete evidence.

   True. Lizbeth is presumed guilty, embarrassed in front of the class, and punished (has to stay after school) based on the fact that she was near the scene of the alleged crime.

6. The problem is that the task was too difficult for Lizbeth. To cope, Lizbeth attempts to avoid this activity and divert attention away from her academic inadequacies.

True. To address these issues, Lizbeth needs academic empowerment and social empowerment.

Multiple Choice: Which solution will work? A, B, or C

Solution A: Behavior modification with a reward

To solve this problem, Lizbeth's teacher should set up a smiley face chart for Lizbeth. Every time she makes it through math class without taking something that is not hers, she will earn a smiley face. At the end of the week, if she has earned a smiley face each day, she can pick something from the teacher's treasure chest (contains toys and trinkets).

Why Solution A will not work for Lizbeth

The first problem with this solution is that the teacher is not sure if Lizbeth is actually taking things or not. Giving or not giving rewards based on circumstantial evidence is not going to help the situation. The teacher needs to find out if Lizbeth is actually taking things or not. If she is taking things we need to uncover the reason, rather than mask the situation with behavior management techniques.

Solution B: Authoritarian rule with a punishment

To solve this problem, the teacher needs to set up a situation that enables her to actually catch Lizbeth in the act of stealing. Once the teacher has proof, Lizbeth should be punished with a severe scolding. This will teach Lizbeth not to steal.

Why Solution B will not work for Lizbeth

Setting up a little sting operation in the classroom is not the most productive use of the teacher's time. The focus is on trying to "catch" Lizbeth being bad. Positive behavior strategies include trying to "catch" students being good. Furthermore, scolding a student like Lizbeth does not solve the problem because Lizbeth seeks attention. While many think that scolding is a negative reinforcement, it is actually a positive reinforcement for students who seek attention. Lizbeth does not discern between types of attention, she only seeks attention. Scolding her gives Lizbeth the attention she seeks and thereby reinforces her misbehavior.

Solution C: Academic empowerment and social empowerment

To solve this problem, Lizbeth needs help building foundations in working with and analyzing data. She needs an assignment that is suited to her level. Lizbeth also needs help with gaining attention for positive behaviors and being a positive member of the classroom community.

Why Solution C will work for Lizbeth

Instruction aimed at Lizbeth's level will academically empower her. Learning how to gain attention in positive ways and becoming a positive part of the classroom community will socially empower Lizbeth.

Essay: Social Empowerment

Possible strategies

Having a conference with Lizbeth to find out what is happening is an important first step. The teacher asked the guidance counselor to join her for this meeting. Together they talked with Lizbeth about how things seemed to be missing and asked her if she knew anything about it. Initially, Lizbeth denied any involvement, then her eyes filled up with tears. She got up and walked around the classroom gathering up the missing items (including the keychain) from strategic hiding places. Lizbeth handed the items to her teacher and said, "I'm sorry." The teacher replied in a concerned voice, "Why did you hide these things?" Lizbeth answered, "I wanted to be the one who found them, so everyone would like me." The teacher and the counselor were surprised, yet they worked to help Lizbeth uncover her desire to get along with her classmates and complimented her for revealing the missing items. Over the next few weeks, Lizbeth met with the counselor to talk through her feelings and to learn strategies for gaining classroom-appropriate attention and being part of a positive classroom community.

One of the strategies that Lizbeth and her teacher found very successful was for Lizbeth to serve as the teacher's helper. Lizbeth distributed supplies and gathered papers. This job gave Lizbeth a lot of attention (and helped the teacher). Initially, Lizbeth served as the teacher's helper every day during math time. To give other students a chance to help, Lizbeth then served as the teacher's helper in math on Mondays. This seemed to set Lizbeth up for a successful week and helped her interact in positive ways with her peers.

Class meeting

Class meetings are a great way to build community, empower students, and solve problems. Class meetings give students a forum to share what is on their minds related to the classroom. Successful class meetings have an agenda and allow each person who wants to share have uninterrupted time to do so. Some teachers only have class meetings when there is a problem that needs to be solved. Unfortunately, some students may interpret the class meeting as a punishment (something that has to be done because the class was bad). Class meetings need to be part of weekly or bi-weekly plans with a way for students to add topics to the agenda as needed. The agenda can be separated into four sections; compliments, updates, issues, and potential solutions.

During a class meeting a few weeks after Lizbeth's conference with her teacher and the counselor, several students shared compliments about how things were no longer missing in the classroom. They celebrated their feelings of satisfaction with this. The students also shared that they thought Lizbeth was doing a great job as the teacher's helper in math class.

Community

The class meetings helped create a positive classroom environment because each meeting served as a forum for students' opinions to be shared, used, and valued. These meetings also helped the class work together to solve problems.

The teacher and students incorporated some additional changes to help build a positive classroom community. They redesigned the group meeting place so that everyone could sit in a circle. The new arrangement enabled the students to see each other. This replaced the "rows" seating that only allowed the students to see the teacher and the backs of their classmates' heads.

The class also created a "Room 3" cheer that they chanted together each morning: "Who are we? Room Three! What do we do? Work together! Who is the best? Room Three! Who is that? You and me!" Developing and reciting the cheer highlighted the team spirit and working together.

Conflict resolution

Even though we work to establish a positive classroom community, conflicts can still arise. When this happens, we should help students use conflict resolution strategies. Ask students to talk to each other about the problem. If someone is angry, there may need to be a cool down time before engaging in this process. The teacher should ask the students if they want to talk to each other alone or if they want the teacher to be present or if they would prefer another student to be present. Each person involved in the conflict should have adequate time to share his opinions and feelings. If the students cannot reach resolution, the teacher (or peer) needs to help them. Guiding students through the process of sharing opinions and feelings and reaching resolution is important not only for the classroom but for life outside of the classroom, too!

Essay: Academic Empowerment

Formative assessment

To find out how to academically empower Lizbeth, the teacher uses a formative assessment. The students are studying data analysis. The teacher uses this formative assessment to find out what Lizbeth knows about bar graphs.

Name _Lizbeth_

Ms. Smith's class will get a new pet. The students collected data about what kind of pet to have in the classroom.

Goldfish		4
Hamster		10
Snake		2
Turtle		7

The students made a graph of the data. Yikes! Several parts of the graph are missing. Add the missing parts of the bar graph.

Lizbeth's responses indicate that she does not know how to transfer data from a table to a bar graph. She does write the correct amounts, but she does not use the bars to show the data. She does not add the category labels, axes labels, numeric increments, or a title for the graph. Clearly, Lizbeth is struggling with bar graphs. The teacher can work with Lizbeth at her level to build her understanding.

Meaningful feedback

Teacher	Lizbeth, let's make a graph using actual objects.
Lizbeth	What do you mean?
Teacher	Well, I have a can of plastic bugs and a graph template.
Lizbeth	Should I sort the bugs?
Teacher	Good idea.
Lizbeth	Where should I put them on the graph?
Teacher	We want the bugs to be organized.
Lizbeth	So I should put them in rows?
Teacher	Yes. Each bug represents a piece of data.
Lizbeth	I have all the bugs in the right rows.
Teacher	What should we call each row?
Lizbeth	Bugs.
Teacher	How are the bugs different?
Lizbeth	These are spiders.
Teacher	Great description. We will call this row "Spiders" and write it down.
Lizbeth	This row should be called "Ants" and this row should be called "Flies."
Teacher	You have labeled all of the rows in this horizontal bar graph.
Lizbeth	What's next?
Teacher	What else do you think we need?
Lizbeth	We need numbers.
Teacher	Yes!
Lizbeth	(after writing the numeric increments) Are we done?
Teacher	Almost. What would you call spiders, ants, and flies?
Lizbeth	Types of bugs.
Teacher	Yes. We can add that axis label right here.
Lizbeth	Does the other side need a label?

Teacher	Yes. What do you think we should call it?
Lizbeth	It is the number of bugs. I will write it.
Teacher	We only need one more thing.
Lizbeth	What's that?
Teacher	A title for the whole graph.
Lizbeth	I'll call it My Graph.
Teacher	It is your graph. Will you also add what the graph is about?
Lizbeth	OK. How about Lizbeth's Bugs?
Teacher	Sounds like a good title.

The feedback offered to Lizbeth helped her increase her knowledge and comfort level with the content. The teacher used actual objects to represent the data to help Lizbeth learn how to organize the data, better matching her learning style. The teacher's questions, prompts, and guidance helped Lizbeth understand more about how data are organized into a bar graph.

Productive instruction

The teacher works with Lizbeth and several other students working at a similar level. The teacher shows the students grid paper and a small bag full of coins. The teacher invites the students to make a bar graph using the actual coins. Based on the knowledge gained from the meaningful feedback, Lizbeth is able to take a leadership role with the group. She asks questions and makes suggestions as the group creates the bar graph with all of the necessary components. After the graph is complete, the teacher demonstrates how to depict the same data using pictures of coins. Together they create a bar graph of the same data, using "stamped" pictures of the coins. The students analyze the two bar graphs and Lizbeth announces that both graphs show the same data. The teacher then introduces a third way to show the same data. The students will use a symbol to represent each coin. The students decide that they want to use a circle as the symbol to represent each coin in this bar graph. The bar graph of the same data is constructed using symbols instead of actual coins or stamped pictures of coins.

After some discussion about each graph, the teacher gives each pair of students in the group a piece of grid paper and a baggie of coins (different values). She invites them to construct their own bar graphs using a symbol of their choice. As the students work on the task, the teacher facilitates and answers questions. Some of the students use X's to represent the coins. Others color in the squares on the grid to represent the coins. Lizbeth and her partner decide to use stars to represent the coins. The teacher asks Lizbeth why she chose to use stars as the symbol in her bar graph. Lizbeth responds, "Because I am a math star now."

Final thoughts

The mini-lesson is powerful, productive instruction for Lizbeth and the other students. The teacher strategically and successfully moves the students through the levels of understanding graphing—actual objects, pictures of objects, symbols representing objects. Lizbeth is able to gain attention in productive ways as she helps the other students. Lizbeth's confidence level increases. She no longer needs to take and hide her classmates' belongings because she has learned how to gain attention in ways that help the classroom community.

Disinterested Diondre

Diondre is a bright student in upper elementary school. Unfortunately, Diondre will do only the bare minimum of what is required even though he is very capable. This is very frustrating to his teacher. What's more, he acts indifferent when he is reprimanded or "called on the carpet." Today, Diondre has arrived to class with homework partially complete and has spent the last fifteen minutes accomplishing nothing on his in-class assignment. His teacher told Diondre that he will miss recess, again, if he does not finish the assignment. Diondre's response was, "I don't care."

Problem Sources: True or False

1. This problem is Diondre's fault. He is lazy. If he were motivated, everything would be fine.

   False. Diondre is not lazy.

2. This problem is Diondre's parents' fault. They do not require anything of their son. He gets away with doing "nothing."

   False. Blaming Diondre's parents does "nothing" to help solve the problem.

3. The problem is that Diondre has ADD (attention-deficit disorder).

   True. Diondre does have ADD. The real problem is that his ADD is currently undiagnosed. Teachers should not give medical diagnoses. Even if the teacher suspects a biochemical condition, the teacher should not share this with the parents. Instead, the teacher should share concerns, evidence, and attempted strategies with the parents. The teacher should also consult the school's special educational team to gather more information. The team may suggest further testing and request a medical diagnosis. Ultimately, it is the parent who decides how to proceed regarding a medical diagnosis.

4. The problem is Diondre has no friends. If he had friends, he would be more involved in math class.

   False. Diondre does have friends. His friends do not cause him to be more involved in math class.

5. The problem is Diondre's teacher does not use strategies that help motivate him or help him concentrate or become more involved with the math. Instead, the teacher uses "missing recess" as a punishment.

   True. This punishment has proved to be ineffective.

6. The problem is that Diondre has trouble focusing on his work. This issue is compounded by the fact that the work is actually too easy for him.

   True. To address these issues, Diondre needs learning empowerment and academic empowerment.

Multiple Choice: Which Solution Will Work? A, B, or C

Solution A: Behavior modification with consequences and attached points

To solve this problem, Diondre's teacher needs to impose consequences with attached points. If Diondre brings his completed homework to class, he earns ten points. If only half of his homework is complete, he earns five points. The points earned will be based on how much of his homework is complete. He will also earn up to ten points on his in-class assignment. Diondre can earn up to 20 points each day! If Diondre does not bring his homework to class, he will need to subtract ten points. Likewise, if he does not do anything on his in-class assignment, he will subtract ten points. When Diondre earns 100 points, he can have lunch with his teacher.

Why Solution A will not work for Diondre

While there is some great math going on with all of these points, this solution is really pointless. Diondre already completes parts of his homework and parts of his in-class assignments, so he will earn some points each day without making the slightest change in his behavior. Not to mention the value of the grand prize—Does Diondre want to have lunch with his teacher? Another interesting question—Does completed homework and completed in-class work imply accuracy or just something written on the paper?

Solution B: Authoritarian rule with a punishment

To solve this problem, Diondre needs to go to study hall every time he fails to bring completed homework or fails to complete the in-class assignment. This will help him remember to do his homework and class assignments. If he forgets, he will have a place and time to complete his work.

Why Solution B will not work for Diondre

While many educators view study hall as a place where students can complete work, many students view study hall as a punishment. Not to mention the fact that having "time" and a "place" to do the work will not help Diondre complete the work because he already has time and a place and the work is not getting done.

Solution C: Academic empowerment and learning empowerment

To solve this problem, Diondre's teacher needs to address his academic needs and his learning needs. Diondre should have instruction at his level and be encouraged to use learning processes that are beneficial to him.

Why Solution C will work for Diondre

By focusing on both his academic needs and his learning needs, the teacher can help Diondre productively engage in learning.

———————•———————

Essay: Learning Empowerment

Possible strategies

Diondre's lack of attention to the task most commonly occurs when the teacher is not nearby. The teacher should strategically locate himself near Diondre as often as possible. Using this close proximity strategy will improve Diondre's time on task. However, this strategy, alone, will not solve Diondre's issues.

If we truly want to help Diondre be successful, it is necessary to uncover the reasons why Diondre does only the bare minimum and acts indifferent.

The teacher and Diondre need to talk about what is happening. The teacher should explain to Diondre that the goal is to help him and ask how this can be done. Most students want to know that their teacher cares about them and that their teacher is willing to help.

During the discussion, Diondre shared with his teacher that he is having trouble "thinking." He shared that he looks at a math problem, thinks of the answer, and then cannot concentrate enough to get the complete answer on the paper. Diondre added that this gives him a headache, so he just starts thinking about something else and drawing pictures in his mind. Before he knows it, the class is over and his work is incomplete. The teacher complimented Diondre for taking the risk to share this information and highlighted his ability to describe what is happening to him. The teacher asked Diondre if he had shared any of this with his parents or other teachers. Diondre said he had not because it was hard to explain and kind of embarrassing. The teacher asked Diondre if he would be willing to talk to his parents about it. Diondre said he would if the teacher would be there. The teacher said that he would be happy to do so. The teacher also shared with Diondre that he wanted to consult with some other teachers about how best to help him. The teacher explained that the school has experts that may be able to help uncover why this is happening to Diondre. Diondre was pleased with the idea.

The teacher should also consider asking Diondre about his sight. Is he having trouble seeing? Is part of the concentration problem related to his vision? If so, Diondre should have vision screening.

Multiple intelligences

The teacher decided to give Diondre a multiple-intelligences survey. The survey revealed that Diondre has two dominant intelligences: "number smart" and "picture smart." The teacher talked with Diondre about the results, and together they brainstormed some ways that they could incorporate this information into Diondre's learning process. They decided to give Diondre a personal dry erase board and marker to see if drawing a picture of the math problem would help him concentrate. They also decided to allow Diondre to go to a section of the classroom chalkboard to draw a depiction of the math problem, if he felt like this would help him refocus. These strategies were evaluated at the end of the week. Both the teacher and Diondre noted that the accommodations were definitely helping Diondre. Diondre asked if he could also use some graphic organizer templates so that he could better see his thoughts and ideas as he worked on various math problems. Of course the teacher agreed that they should give it a try.

Essay: Academic Empowerment

Formative assessment

Using a simple formative assessment, the teacher learns a great deal about Diondre's understanding of perimeter.

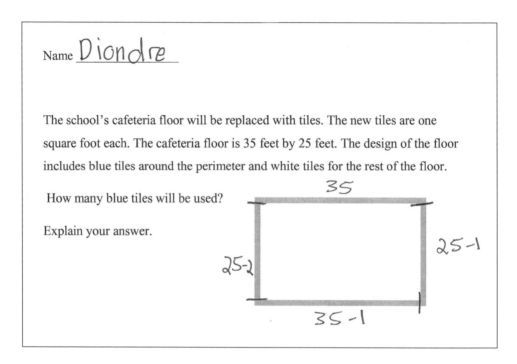

While Diondre did not complete the task, he did show a high level of understanding about perimeter and problem solving. He knows that two sides are 35 feet and two sides are 25 feet. He clearly marks on the diagram of the cafeteria floor which tiles are counted with each side. Without using a technique like this, a student might simply add 35 + 25 + 35 + 25 or multiply and add (2 × 35) + (2 × 25). But Diondre understands that this will produce an error. When Diondre writes 25 – 1 he is indicating that one of the tiles on that side has already been counted. Likewise 35 – 1 shows that one time has already been counted and 25 – 2 explains that 2 of those tiles have already been counted. It really is a clever way to draw and describe the math thinking that Diondre is using. Diondre will need a challenge because he already knows this level of content.

Meaningful feedback and productive instruction

Using the same cafeteria floor problem, the teacher engaged Diondre in a more challenging task.

Teacher	Diondre, what if the cafeteria floor were made using concentric rectangles that alternated blue and white.
Diondre	What are concentric rectangles?
Teacher	Rectangles that share the same center.
Diondre	Do you mean rectangles inside of rectangles?
Teacher	Yes.
Diondre	So it would go blue, white, blue, white, and so on until the center?
Teacher	Yes. I like how you described that.
Diondre	Can I draw it?
Teacher	Of course. You may want to use graph paper.
Diondre	That's a good idea. I need a piece that is 35 by 25.
Teacher	How many squares make up the area?
Diondre	Easy. *Diondre puts the equation into the calculator.* It is $35 \times 25 = 875$.
Teacher	So how many blue tiles will you need?
Diondre	I need to draw this out. Can you give me a few minutes?
Teacher	Yes. I'll be back to check on you in a bit. Let me know if you need any help focusing.
	Diondre worked on the task for ten minutes. He was completely engaged in the task using his number smart and picture smart intelligences.
Teacher	How's it going?
Diondre	I almost have it. Take a look at this.
	Diondre shows his teacher the drawing of the cafeteria floor.

Teacher	Wow, Diondre! That is fantastic. Tell me about it.
Diondre	I started by drawing each row on the graph paper. When I got to the center and it was just a row of 11 tiles, I thought I was wrong. But then I realized that it is still a rectangle even if it is only one tile tall.
Teacher	You are right.
Diondre	Then I started counting from the outside in and I started to lose my concentration. So I thought about how the outside blue rectangle was related to the next white rectangle inside of it.
Teacher	What did you find out?
Diondre	I already knew the outside blue was $35 + (25-1) + (35-1) + (25 - 2) = 116$. The white rectangle is two less tall and wide than the outside blue. So it is $33 + (23-1) + (33-1) + (23-2) = 108$.
Teacher	Very cool.
Diondre	Yeah. I know. It gets even better because each one is eight less than the one before. See my list on the chalkboard?

Diondre shows the teacher his work.

Blue: 116	White: 60
White: 108	Blue: 52
Blue: 100	White: 44
White: 92	Blue: 36
Blue: 84	White: 28
White: 76	Blue: 11
Blue: 68	

Diondre	I knew I was right when I got to 11 because that matched the picture. And I added them all up and it was 875, the same 35 × 25. That's 467 blue tiles and 408 white tiles.
Teacher	Diondre, I am really impressed with your work. You used your multiple intelligences and stepped up to a big math challenge. You stuck with it and completed everything!
Diondre	I am proud of me.
Teacher	I am proud of you, too. For homework tonight I want you to take a piece of graph paper and make a different tile design and tell how many of each color tile will be needed.
Diondre	OK. I will.

The meaningful feedback and productive instruction offered by the teacher was extremely powerful. Using guiding questions and prompts, the teacher gave just the right amount of support and challenge. The task was targeted at Diondre's academic level. The task also included ways for Diondre to stay focused by using his multiple intelligences. Diondre was successful even when working on his own because the teacher gave him the tools, set the challenge and expectations, and offered help if needed. Intentionally, the homework assignment was directly related to what Diondre had successfully accomplished on his own in class!

Final thoughts

The teacher did meet with Diondre and his parents. He also consulted the school's special educational team. Later, the teacher and the parents met with the educational management team. Eventually, a medical diagnosis was given by Diondre's pediatrician and an Individual Educational Plan (IEP) was developed for Diondre. He also now wears glasses.

Mouthy Maria

Maria is mouthy and sassy. She thinks she knows everything. Today, right in the middle of the lesson on fractions, Maria called out, "I already know that!" The teacher tried to remain calm saying, "No, Maria, you don't. Now please listen." Maria yelled, "Yes. I do! I learned that last year." Annoyed and insulted, the teacher reached for a behavior referral form, marked the box labeled *disrespectful behavior* and wrote in the comments section, *rude to the teacher and disruptive to the class*. She handed the form to Maria and announced "Take this to the office." Maria took the form, rolled her eyes, and headed for the door. The teacher responded, "Don't roll your eyes at me!" Maria said under her breath, "You're retarded" and left the classroom.

Problem Sources: True or False

1. The problem is that Maria is a condescending, spiteful little pain-in-the-neck.

   False. While Maria's behaviors do annoy the teacher, Maria is actually bright and confident.

2. The problem is that Maria's parents spend all of their time kowtowing to Maria.

   False. While Maria's parents rarely challenge her behavior, they do not kneel in submission to her. In either case, this is not the key to solving Maria's classroom behavior.

3. Maria has Generalized Anxiety Disorder. She is obsessed with her grades, which causes her to be irritable.

   False. Maria does not have Generalized Anxiety Disorder.

4. The problem is that Maria thinks she is better than all of her classmates. Therefore, no one likes her.

   False. There are *many* students in the class that like, even admire, Maria.

5. The problem is that the teacher over-reacts to Maria.

   True. When Maria says, "I learned that last year" the teacher takes it as an insult. It may actually be true that Maria learned the information last year. Instead of engaging in an argument with Maria, the teacher needs to use more productive, less reactive ways to respond to Maria's words and actions.

6. The problem is that the content is too easy for Maria, and the teacher and Maria need to learn mutual respect.

   True. To address these issues, Maria needs academic empowerment and emotional empowerment.

Multiple Choice: Which Solution Will Work? A, B, or C

Solution A: Behavior modification using a class conduct chart

To solve this problem, the teacher needs to use a Class Conduct Chart. The chart includes attached pockets (paper envelopes) labeled with each student's name. Cards are inserted into the pockets to display the level of disruptive behavior. Green cards are good. Everyone starts with a green card. If someone, like Maria, displays a disruptive behavior, the green card is replaced by a yellow card in that student's pocket on the chart. Yellow cards represent "warning." If the student displays another disruptive behavior, the yellow card is replaced by a red card. Red cards are bad. If a student is "red carded" a note is sent home to parents.

Why Solution A will not work for Maria

Classroom Conduct Charts are problematic for several reasons. The chart evokes fear in some well-behaving students. They are afraid of yellow and red cards. The fear actually distracts these students from the learning process. Other students, like Maria, are not afraid of the cards because they don't really care. A note home to Maria's parents does nothing to change her behavior. Furthermore, conduct charts can be exhausting to the teacher who has to spend time going to the chart and changing cards. If the teacher demands that students change their own cards when told to do so, the focus is on humiliation. The conduct chart can become the center of attention. Everyone is analyzing the chart to see who is in the "warning zone" or "red zone." We want students to be focused on learning, not on negative behaviors.

Solution B: Authoritarian rule with a potential punishment

To solve this problem, the teacher needs to use "Detention Hangman." If a student misbehaves in any way, that student's name is written on the board and the gallows are drawn below. Each infraction results in another part of the offender's body being drawn in the gallows. The head is drawn first, then the torso, followed by lines to represent the arms and legs. Gallows for different students can be constructed at the same time depending upon how many students are misbehaving. When all the parts of the body are drawn, the student is considered "hanged" and must serve detention. A variation to this strategy is to allow the student more chances by including eyes, a nose, and a frown on the face. Another variation of this idea is to use check marks instead of the hanging gallows and body parts. The first infraction earns the student's name on the board. Each additional infraction is recorded with a check mark by that student's name. The teacher decides the various punishments for each amount of check marks (these consequences should be posted).

Why Solution B will not work for Maria

Maria likes to play detention hangman. She enjoys watching the irritated teacher add parts on the hangman diagram. Maria pushes the teacher and stops right before the last "leg" (or "frown" depending upon the version of detention hangman that is being implemented). This strategy gives control of the classroom to Maria and actually serves to promote misbehavior. The focus on math is lost because all eyes are on the pending doom of each student represented by a hangman diagram. Most students are distracted. Some students (including Maria) are entertained at the expense of the teacher. Detention hangman is a ridiculous strategy. The more common check marks approach is not much better. Students are distracted, entertained, afraid, or indifferent. Note: I once watched in disbelief and horror as a teacher continued to add check mark after check mark beside a child's name because he could not find his paper. She finally ran out of room on the chalkboard. Another Note: One of my teachers used detention hangman and I played the game much like Maria (I'm sorry Mrs. Hubbard).

Solution C: Academic empowerment and emotional empowerment

To solve this problem, Maria needs to be challenged academically. She needs math content that is aimed at her level. Maria and her teacher need to set mutual limits and learn how to engage in mutual respect.

Why Solution C will work for Maria

Targeted instruction will academically empower Maria. Learning how to set mutual limits and engage in mutual respect will emotionally empower Maria (and her teacher).

Essay: Emotional Empowerment

Possible strategies

One strategy that the teacher could implement involves using a distraction. The distraction technique could be used when Maria first calls out. Perhaps the teacher strategically asks some of the students to stand and move. The teacher could say, "Students at Table 3, please stand and walk over to the math manipulatives area and gather the supplies you will need for today's tasks." The standing and moving serve to take attention away from Maria's calling out. Adding a redirection to the distraction strategy makes it more effective. While the students are gathering supplies, the teacher can offer Maria a quick, private redirection. She may say, "Maria, remember you are trying not to call out. Raise your hand if you want to tell me something." Or "You don't have to call out. Just let me know that you want to tell me something and I will come over to you as soon as I can."

Another way to help Maria learn not to call out is for the teacher to give a reminder signal. Maria is so used to calling out that she hardly notices when she does it. The teacher and Maria should set the goal of reducing the frequency of calling out and decide upon a signal together. The purpose of the signal is to help Maria gain control of her calling-out issue. We also need to teach Maria to discern when calling out is appropriate and when it is not. If the teacher is explaining the assignment, it is not appropriate to call out. However, if the teacher says, "Are you ready for some fun, class?" It is appropriate for all of the students (including Maria) to call out "Yes!"

The teacher could help Maria and the other students by cupping the back of her ear when she wants the class to know that is appropriate to call out. These and all strategies should constantly be evaluated for effectiveness (including finding the point at which the strategies are no longer needed).

Additionally, and more important, the teacher needs to figure out why Maria's calling out irritates her and why Maria calls out. Is the teacher annoyed because Maria calls out? Or is the teacher frustrated due to what Maria is actually saying when she calls out? In this case, it is both. Also, why Maria is calling out? Is she bored? Is she seeking attention? Is she trying to irritate the teacher? In this case the first two are true and the third is sometimes true.

When Maria calls out, the teacher feels interrupted and disrespected. The teacher is insulted when Maria claims she already knows the information or she learned it in the previous grade. She feels like Maria is poking holes in her instruction. The teacher and Maria need to have a candid conversation. During this conversation, the teacher can share some of her feelings. She may say, "Maria, I know you are smart. It distracts me when you call out. I feel like you are not respecting me or my work." Maria may respond, "I feel like you are not respecting me when you teach something that I already know." This is the beginning of a frank discussion that could actually change the behavior of both the teacher and Maria.

Mutual respect

Arguing with students, over-reacting with behavior referrals, and yelling at students are disrespectful behaviors from the teacher. Criticizing the teacher, rolling her eyes, and name calling (even if no one else heard) are disrespectful behaviors from the student. Both the teacher and the student need to make a commitment and develop a plan to be more respectful. To initiate the process the teacher should ask Maria what she could do to show respect to her. Maria should ask the teacher what she can do to show respect to her. They should act upon these requests (given that the requests are appropriate and productive) and then evaluate the effectiveness. They may even add further requests of each other. Mutual respect is earned by the parties involved. Each day students and teachers have the opportunity to share positive feelings, words, and actions about and with one another.

The teacher should offer appropriate, non-distracting ways Maria can let her know if the content is too easy. Perhaps Maria can write a journal entry that includes evidence of her claim that she already knows. For example, if the teacher is teaching how to order fractions, Maria can explain how to order fractions and give an example in her journal. There should be a designated time when the teacher looks at Maria's journal entry and explains how what she is teaching is different or provides her with a more challenging aspect to the task. Maria shows respect to her teacher by not interrupting or distracting her and the teacher shows respect by providing Maria with appropriate instruction.

Essay: Academic Empowerment

Formative assessment

To find out how to academically empower Maria, the teacher uses a formative assessment involving comparing and ordering fractions and mixed numbers.

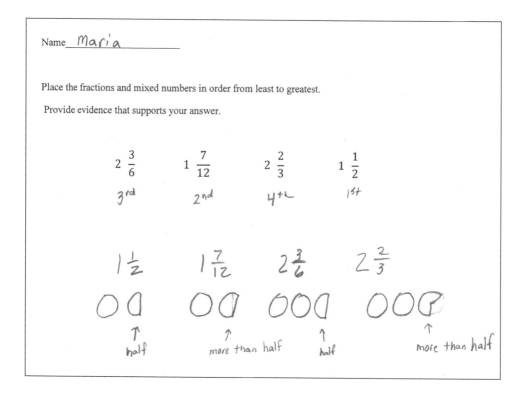

Name Maria

Place the fractions and mixed numbers in order from least to greatest.

Provide evidence that supports your answer.

$$2\frac{3}{6} \qquad 1\frac{7}{12} \qquad 2\frac{2}{3} \qquad 1\frac{1}{2}$$

3rd   2nd   4th   1st

$$1\frac{1}{2} \qquad 1\frac{7}{12} \qquad 2\frac{3}{6} \qquad 2\frac{2}{3}$$

half   more than half   half   more than half

Maria has a high level of understanding of how to compare and order these fractions and mixed numbers. Her response is completely accurate and her evidence (pictures and words) explains her thinking and provides insight into her strong number sense. Maria needs more challenging material because she already knows the content.

Meaningful feedback

Teacher   Maria, I saw on your preassessment that you already know a lot about comparing and ordering fractions and mixed numbers.

Maria	Yeah. I just compared them to a half each time.
Teacher	That was clever of you.
Maria	Thanks.
Teacher	Would you like to try a similar task with improper fractions?
Maria	What's an improper fraction?
Teacher	I would like to teach you.
Maria	OK.
Teacher	It is an improper fraction when the numerator is greater than or equal to the denominator.
Maria	Can you give me an example?
Teacher	Let's try 5/4.
Maria	Oh, I get it, because it is more than one.
Teacher	Right. And 4/4 is an improper fraction, too.
Maria	But not 3/4.
Teacher	Correct.
Maria	What about mixed numbers? Are they improper fractions?
Teacher	Mixed numbers can be proper or improper.
Maria	Cool.
Teacher	Indeed. While I work with some other students, I want you to create a list of five proper fractions and five improper fractions. Then put the fractions in order.
Maria	Can I use mixed numbers, too?
Teacher	Of course! One more thing, I want you to include one intentional mistake for me to try to find.
Maria	Awesome. Get ready for the challenge!
Teacher	I'll be ready.

In this verbal exchange, the teacher provides meaningful feedback that teaches Maria a new concept and invites her to engage in more challenging material. Both the teacher and Maria are respectful and actually appear to enjoy the teaching-learning process. The teacher uses an interesting twist when she invites Maria to include an intentional mistake that she will try to find. This idea encourages Maria to use fractions and mixed numbers that are close to being equal, which requires more thinking than if she used fractions and mixed numbers that are far from being equal. After Maria finished the task, she asked her teacher if she would consider trying to find her intentional error as her "homework" for the night. The teacher agreed.

Productive instruction

The teacher worked with a small group of students (including Maria) that were ready for more challenging content. She taught them a game called Lucky Ducky, Ducks in a Row. (This game appears in *Math intervention: Building number power with formative assessment, differentiation, and games—Grades 3-5* by J. Taylor-Cox, 2009, Larchmont, NY: Eye on Education. Copyright 2009 by Eye on Education. Reprinted with permission.) The game involves students racing to put a fraction, a mixed number, and an improper fraction in order. Students take turns picking duck cards (with the fractions and mixed numbers on them) and writing them in order on individual dry erase boards. After the students play the game for a bit, the teacher adds an interesting twist. Now they need to draw a number line and not only place the fractions and mixed numbers in order, but also consider how these should be spaced on the number line. The teacher demonstrates the first round and the students discuss why the placements make sense. The teacher decides the students should work in pairs to increase the math discourse and invite more cooperative problem solving. The students, including Maria, have fun as they meet the challenges given by the teacher.

Final thoughts

Math games make learning fun for many students, especially when the teacher adjusts the game to the appropriate level for students. Maria and her teacher worked to continue to build their relationship through mutual respect. The teacher offered academic challenges to Maria and Maria focused on meeting those challenges instead of misbehaving. The great part is that Maria learned from her teacher. She started thinking of ways that she could challenge herself at times. The teacher encouraged Maria to continue to do so, all the while providing productive instruction for Maria and the rest of the students. The classroom changed. Everyone worked to build mutual respect, offering emotional and academic empowerment for all.

4

Middle School and High School Students and Situations

The following chapter includes different math classroom situations and related solutions involving middle and high school students. While these scenarios are presented in secondary settings, it is important to recognize that similar misbehaviors can occur with younger students. Additionally, misbehaviors transcend gender, race, and culture. The scenarios presented are not intended to stereotype in any way. The goal is to look at specific misbehaviors and provide productive solutions.

Prepare to meet...Daydreamer Dewain, Texting Tashi, Felix the Fighter, Rude Rashanda, Carlos the Clown, Sleepy Susanna, and Arrogant Anna

Daydreamer Dewain

Dewain is an Algebra 1 "repeater" student. His Algebra teacher is frustrated because Dewain never completes his homework and does not pay attention in class. He just daydreams the class period away. Most of the time, Dewain is flipping his pencil, drumming his fingers, or tapping his foot while he stares off into space. He is irresponsible, unfocussed, and careless. Consequently, Dewain is failing Algebra 1, again. Dewain's mother has met with his teacher several times, but is unwilling to consent to any special services or testing.

Problem Sources: True or False

1. This problem is Dewain's fault. If he would just take responsibility for his homework, stop daydreaming, and pay attention in class, he would be fine.

   False. Blaming Dewain does nothing to help him succeed in Algebra I. If Dewain knew how to take responsibility given the circumstances, he would have most likely already done so. This does not imply that Dewain should not be responsible for his learning. Ultimately, we want students to be responsible for their learning, but simply telling them to do so rarely results in any change. In this case, Dewain is not doing his homework because he doesn't know how. Likewise, he is daydreaming because this is his way of dealing with the reality that he does not understand the math.

2. This problem is Dewain's mother's fault. She should have him tested so he can get the help he needs. What is she so afraid of?

   False. Blaming Dewain's mother does not solve the problem. She most likely needs someone to help her understand the testing process so that her fears of Dewain being labeled and/or stigmatized can be alleviated. Dewain's mother needs to build a working relationship with someone from the school so that she can develop a higher level of trust.

3. The problem is that Dewain has Depressive Disorder. He needs anti-depressants to help him.

   False. Dewain is not depressed and teachers are not qualified to give medical diagnoses (unless they are moonlighting as pediatricians). Furthermore, medicine does not solve all problems and there are often issues with side effects and dosages.

4. The problem is that Dewain's peers distract him from paying attention and completing his homework.

   False. Dewain's difficulties are not due to his peers. Dewain's problems with focusing in class and completing his homework are because the work is too difficult for him.

5. The problem is that Dewain's principal will not suspend him from school because he has not "harmed himself or others."

   False. Expecting the principal to take severe disciplinary actions because of lack of homework completion and a student's inattentiveness in class is inappropriate and unproductive. The teacher needs to address these issues with Dewain in the classroom.

6. The problem is that the curriculum is too difficult for Dewain. He lacks the foundations in algebraic thinking that are needed for this class.

   True. To address these issues, Dewain needs academic empowerment and specific intervention.

———◆———

Multiple Choice: Which Solution Will Work? A, B, or C

Solution A: Behavior modification with a reward

To solve this problem, Dewain's teacher needs to put him on a contract. He can earn points for completing his homework and paying attention in class. If he earns enough points, he can receive a "free homework pass."

Why Solution A will not work for Dewain:

Dewain has had dozens of contracts over the course of his school career. Sometimes the teacher did not remember to record the information. Sometimes Dewain failed to bring his contract to class. Even if Dewain remembers the contract and the information is recorded, the truth is that Dewain does not care about the "reward." The reward itself is also problematic. It is a contradiction to have a student complete homework for the reward of not having to complete homework.

Solution B: Authoritarian rule with a punishment

To solve this problem, Dewain's teacher needs to toughen up on him. She needs to demand that he complete his homework and pay attention in class. If he doesn't follow the rules, he cannot be in her class.

Why Solution B will not work for Dewain:

Dewain has had plenty of teachers in the past who have unsuccessfully made such demands. It is difficult to demand that a student complete homework because the teacher is not there to supervise (let alone help) with the homework. Demands to "pay attention" are typically just as unsuccessful. Some authoritarians are able to make students "act like" they are paying attention by displaying certain behaviors, but this is no guarantee that the student is actually paying attention. In addition, the teacher should not state that any students would not be allowed in her class.

Solution C: Academic empowerment and learning empowerment

To solve this problem, Dewain's teacher needs to uncover Dewain's academic needs and learning style. Dewain actually needs some scaffolding because the in-class and homework material is too difficult for him. He has some gaps in learning and has already developed misconceptions that need to be addressed. He also needs approaches to learning that encourage his individual learning style.

Why Solution C will work for Dewain

By uncovering Dewain's academic needs, his teacher can help Dewain be successful. With scaffolded instruction, the teacher can help Dewain correct misconceptions and fill the gaps in his knowledge. Knowledge of and attention to Dewain's learning style will further the solution.

Essay: Learning Empowermen

Possible strategies

One of the strategies Dewain's teacher could implement is hurdle help. This strategy calls for the teacher to work with Dewain for a brief time and then leave him to complete a portion of the assignment on his own. When the teacher returns, Dewain can ask questions or seek advice based on what he has accomplished up to that point.

Another strategy that should be implemented is small group instruction. The teacher can work with Dewain and a few other students who are working at a similar level. The small group instruction will be targeted to meet the immediate academic needs of the students.

Learning styles

After giving Dewain a learning styles inventory, the teacher learns that Dewain is a visual/tactile learner. To empower Dewain, the teacher demonstrates how to model and draw an algebraic pattern with algebra tiles. Dewain creates models and illustrations for additional terms in the pattern. Afterward, Dewain, on his own, solves other similar problems presented in the textbook. Dewain's teacher assigns homework to Dewain, and several other students working at a similar level, based on the work that they have just completed. They will develop their own algebraic patterns and corresponding expressions. The key to instruction of this type is to start with the student's learning style strength (to build success and confidence) and move the student toward understanding the material in other formats.

Essay: Academic Empowerment

To find out what Dewain's gaps and misconceptions are, the teacher uses a high-quality, yet simple formative assessment.

Formative assessment

Dewain's teacher gives him a formative assessment to find out what he knows about algebraic patterns. Specifically, she wants to learn the degree of understanding Dewain has about using expressions to solve and describe growing patterns.

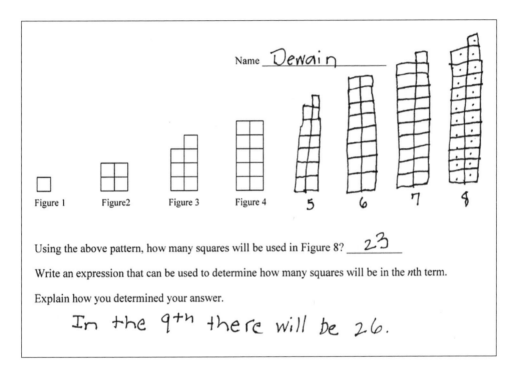

Name __Dewain__

Figure 1   Figure2   Figure 3   Figure 4   5   6   7   8

Using the above pattern, how many squares will be used in Figure 8? ___23___

Write an expression that can be used to determine how many squares will be in the *n*th term.

Explain how you determined your answer.

In the 9th there will be 26.

Dewain's response to the formative assessment reveals a great deal of information about his current level of knowledge and his ways of thinking. He draws pictures to help him solve the problem, which reveals his visual/tactile learning style. He accurately numbers each figure which shows he understands what he is trying to solve. Figure 5 and Figure 6 are accurate, but Figures 7 and 8 are not. There also seems to be confusion between the concepts of the *n*th term versus the ninth term.

Meaningful feedback

The teacher and Dewain take a look at his responses on the formative assessment. They engage in meaningful discourse.

Teacher	Tell me about how you solved this problem.
Dewain	I drew pictures.
Teacher	How did you know what to draw?
Dewain	Well, I looked at the ones that were already there.
Teacher	So, how did you know to draw 13 squares in Figure 5?
Dewain	Each one is three more. It is easy. Ten plus three.
Teacher	Using that idea, how many will be next?
Dewain	13 + 3 = 16. See I have 16 there.
Teacher	What's next?
Dewain	16 and 3 more. Nineteen (Dewain counts the squares). Oh, that's where I messed up. I have too many. That makes the last one wrong. But I get it now.
Teacher	So how many squares are in the 8th term?
Dewain	Twenty-two.
Teacher	What's your proof to back up that answer?
Dewain	Everyone gets three bigger.

The feedback offered by Dewain's teacher in this exchange is very meaningful. She guides Dewain as he verifies and corrects portions of his work. He is very focused and is able to accurately explain his answers. When the teacher asks for "proof" she is setting the stage for what she will teach next—how to express an algebraic pattern.

Productive instruction

The teacher opts for small group instruction because there are several other students who are struggling with how to write an expression to determine the nth term. She builds on Dewain's answer, "Everyone gets three bigger." The students describe this idea (recursive relationship) in a variety of ways; plus 3, 3 more, and so on. The teacher asks the students to think about all figures in relation to their figure number. For example, how is figure four related to how many squares it has? The students decide that ten is six more than four. They test this idea by asking a question about Figure 3. Is seven six more than three? Of course the answer is no. The teacher guides the students to ask what connection (functional relationship) is applicable to all of the figures and focuses their attention on figures 1 and 2. The students realize that if you multiply the figure number by 3 and then subtract two, you will know the number of squares in that figure. They test this idea on all the other figures and even some figures not included in the example. The teacher asks the students how they could write this idea in an expression. They decide that $3n-2$ appropriately describes the pattern. The teacher informs them that they have just described the nth term.

Final thoughts

Because Dewain's teacher provided academic empowerment and learning empowerment, Dewain was engaged in class and completed his work. There were no problems with Dewain "paying attention" because he was actively involved in the learning. The homework was completed by Dewain because he understood what to do and how to do it.

Texting Tashi

It seems like Tashi is addicted to texting. With her cell phone hidden from the teacher's view, she receives and sends text messages during the entire class period. Two weeks ago the teacher contacted Tashi's father to explain the problem. The teacher was shocked when Tashi's father's response to the telephone conference was to buy Tashi a new cell phone. Today, during Algebra class, the teacher spies Tashi texting under her desk. The teacher strolls around the classroom and comes up behind Tashi, leans in close, and yells, "Put that away!" Startled, Tashi slips her phone in her purse and calls back, "Your breath stinks!" The teacher replies, "Lucky you! You get to smell my breath during detention today." Tashi responds, "Why are you trying to kill me?" The students in the class snicker and jeer. The infuriated teacher announces that the entire class will have detention!

Problem Sources: True or False

1. This problem is Tashi's fault. She is sneaky and mean.

   False. While Tashi was reading a text message, which she is not sup-posed to do during class, her goal was not to be sneaky, rather to receive an important message. Furthermore, Tashi is not mean. She only said those things to the teacher because she was frightened and embarrassed. It was, in fact, the teacher who initiated the "meanness" by sneaking up on Tashi and yelling at her.

2. The problem is Tashi's father. Why in the world would he buy Tashi a new cell phone when the teacher just explained that Tashi is texting during class?

   False. While it does not appear to make sense that Tashi's father bought her a new cell phone, blaming Tashi's father does little to solve the problem. The teacher needs to have an honest conversation with Tashi and her father to understand the situation.

3. The problem is that Tashi has Text Messaging Syndrome. She needs medication so that she will stop obsessing over text messages.

   False. There is a known illness called Text Messaging Syndrome, but the illness involves a repetitive strain injury that may result from overuse of the thumb muscles. Tashi does not have Text Messaging Syndrome.

4. The problem is Tashi's peers. Too many of her friends are texting her during class. Furthermore, Tashi likes to put the teacher down to get the rest of the class to hoot and holler.

   False. Tashi's friends are not the only people text messaging Tashi. The reality is that Tashi's mother has been in the hospital for over a month. Tashi's father and other relatives text Tashi every time they see her mother or hear something about her prognosis. The unfortunate news is that it does not look good for Tashi's mother. Today, when Tashi told the teacher she had bad breath, she was attempting to "save face" because she was embarrassed in front of her peers. She felt that she had to do something; otherwise she would look stupid to everyone.

5. The problem is that the teacher interprets Tashi's behavior as defiant and attempts to gain control by exerting power.

   True. When Tashi is texting during class, the teacher feels that she must stop the misbehavior before things "get out of hand." When Tashi insults her saying she has bad breath, the teacher zings back an insult. The power struggle is in full swing. The other students add to the problem with their jeers and whoops. The teacher takes out her frustration on the entire class and issues the revenge of "Detention for All."

6. The problem is that the curriculum is not interesting to Tashi. In addition to the stress of her mother's illness, Tashi is simply not interested in algebra.

   True. To address these issues, Tashi needs academic empowerment (with personalized interest) and social empowerment.

Multiple Choice: Which Solution Will Work? A, B, or C

Solution A: Authoritarian rule with a zero tolerance policy

To get control of this situation, the teacher needs to employ a zero tolerance classroom policy. If a student is caught texting, the cell phone is confiscated and detention is administered. If the class insults the teacher, the entire class will have detention. These simple steps will alleviate the problems.

Why Solution A will not work for Tasha:

Zero tolerance policies leave no room for exceptions and suffocate the opportunity to understand a specific situation. Tashi needs her cell phone. It is her life-line to her mother's future. Yet, using her cell phone during class is distraction and it is not "fair" to all of the other students who want to use their cell phones. The situation poses a dilemma that will not be resolved via a zero tolerance policy. Furthermore, imposing a policy that encourages the teacher to give an entire class detention because the students "insult" the teacher is not fair to the group of students who do not do anything insulting. They are blamed and punished for something they did not do. Often teachers who give the entire class detention are teachers who do this frequently, thereby proving the fact that the detention is not serving to deter the behavior (and is therefore an ineffective punishment).

Solution B: Behavior modification with reward

To solve this problem, the teacher needs to set up a reward system with Tashi. For every class period that Tashi displays the appropriate behavior, her teacher will reward her by giving her a token for the school store.

Why Solution B will not work for Tasha:

This will not work for Tashi for several reasons. First "appropriate behavior" is not defined. To have any chance of being successful, a behavior modification plan needs to be very clear. The teacher and the student need to know exactly what is expected and what will be rewarded. Another reason this plan will not work for Tashi is that the reward is meaningless to her. She does not shop at the school store and will not use the tokens. In addition, Tashi feels embarrassed when the teacher gives her a token. It is like a dog and pony show.

Solution C: Academic empowerment and social empowerment

To solve this problem, Tashi's teacher needs to focus on Tashi's academic needs, specific interests, and social needs. Tashi needs some help understanding how algebra is part of the real world and will gain further motivation if her interests are tied to the content. The teacher and Tashi need to focus on positive communication.

Why Solution C will work for Tashi

By focusing on Tashi's academic needs, interests, and social needs, her teacher can help Tashi find success. The positive communication needed for Tashi and her teacher will enable Tashi to have some support during her family crisis.

———— • ————

Essay: Social Empowerment

Possible strategies

Because of the nature of the situation, Tashi's teacher could make an exception to the rule about cell phone usage during class (with approval from the school's administration, if there is a school or district policy regarding students using cell phones). Perhaps Tashi's teacher could allow Tashi to check her text messages once or twice during each class period. To avoid the potential snowball effect of everyone wanting the same privilege, Tashi's teacher could grant her a "hall pass to the guidance counselor's office" to leave the classroom for a couple of minutes to check her text messages. Or Tashi's father could inform the guidance counselor if something critical happens regarding Tashi's mother's condition. The counselor could then find Tashi and allow her to come to the office to communicate (voice or text) with her father. Tashi and the teacher should evaluate the effectiveness of these strategies at the end of the week. Did Tashi leave class for only a brief time? Did she overuse the "hall pass?" Did it help Tashi to concentrate more on her class work knowing that she could check her text messages when she needed to do so? Did it help Tashi to know that the guidance counselor will come to get her if something critical happens to her mother? Were these strategies too distracting to Tashi, the teacher, or the rest of the class? These and other questions will help Tashi and the teacher evaluate the effectiveness of the strategies.

Communication

Tashi's teacher needs to open the door for positive communication between her and Tashi. She could ask Tashi to stay after class or see her after school. When they meet, Tashi's teacher could initiate the conversation in this way; "Tashi, it seems like something is really bothering you. Can I help?" When Tashi crosses her arms, slumps in the chair and says, "Nope." The teacher should not take this personally. Tashi is simply protecting herself from pain and humiliation. It is hard for Tashi to forget how she felt when the teacher screamed at her. The teacher should take responsibility for the mistake.

Teacher	"Tashi, the first thing I should do is apologize. I am sorry that I screamed at you today. I was frustrated about the texting."
Tashi	Sorry. I text a lot.
Teacher	Thank you. Is there something important that you are texting?
Tashi	Yes.
Teacher	Is it really important?
Tashi	Yes. *(Tashi's eyes are filled with tears)*.
Teacher	It seems like you are dealing with a very difficult situation. What if when you really need to text, you just come and get this hall pass from my desk *(teacher shows Tashi the hall pass)*. I will let your guidance counselor know.
Tashi	Thanks.
Teacher	Tashi, I don't want you to miss a lot of class, so could you limit this to just once or twice during class and only for a couple of minutes at a time?
Tashi	Yes. I can do that.
Teacher	Let's meet at the end of the week and discuss how this works out for you and me.
Tashi	OK.

To further the communication, Tashi's teacher should request a conference with Tashi and her father. The seed for a positive exchange has already been planted because of the meeting with Tashi and the new strategy. After initial greetings, Tashi's father opens the conference by thanking the teacher for giving Tashi a way to text without getting into trouble. The teacher responds that she is concerned about Tashi and wants to help. Tashi and her father then explain that they have a family crisis and that Tashi needs to be available to receive updates. The teacher explains the strategy and parameters that she and Tashi have agreed upon and invites the father to join them for the evaluation. She also reminds both Tashi and her father that she will keep the details about their family crisis confidential unless otherwise instructed by them. Everyone leaves the meeting feeling respected and hopeful.

Essay: Academic Empowerment

To find out Tashi's academic needs, the teacher uses a simple, yet formative assessment.

Formative assessment

Tashi's teacher gives her this formative assessment to find out how she understands the relationships represented in algebraic equations.

Name __Tashi__

The number of people (n) who will go to the basketball game depends on the cost (c), in dollars, of the ticket. Explain how this relationship is represented in the following equation.

$$n = 1,000 - 25c$$

The number of people varies directly with the cost of the ticket. So supposdley, If the ticket is cheaper more people will come. BUT I would not go!

Tashi's response to the formative assessment reveals a great deal of information about Tashi. It appears that Tashi has some understanding of the relationship within the equation, but she needs to increase her understanding of direct variation and to support her response with numeric details.

The last statement invites the teacher to ask Tashi why she would not go to the basketball game. When Tashi explains that she does not like basketball, her teacher decides to give her an interest inventory (to reveal some of Tashi likes and dislikes).

Meaningful feedback

After reviewing Tashi's responses on the interest inventory, the teacher decides to work with Tashi on the same algebraic equation, but with a different real world context.

Teacher	Tashi, I noticed from the interest inventory that you like going to concerts.
Tashi	Yes. I really like the Maxed Out Jumping Beans.
Teacher	What if we change this problem from a basketball game to a concert by the Jumping Beans?
Tashi	The *Maxed Out* Jumping Beans.
Teacher	Yes. The *Maxed Out* Jumping Beans.
Tashi	OK.
Teacher	So, the number of people who attend the Maxed Out Jumping Beans concert depends on the cost in dollars of the ticket. $n = 1{,}000 - 25c$
Tashi	Ok. n is the number of people and c is the cost (in dollars).
Teacher	Yes. So what do we do with that information?
Tashi	Well, you have to think about how many people will go at what price.
Teacher	So what if the cost is $1 per ticket.
Tashi	That would never happen.
Teacher	Why not?
Tashi	Because the Maxed Out Jumping Beans are really good. It would have to cost more than one dollar for a ticket.
Teacher	What if the Maxed Out Jumping Beans are selling tickets only to people who already paid to become members of their fan club?
Tashi	Like after a $100 membership, you can buy cheap tickets?
Teacher	Yes. Exactly.
Tashi	OK. That might happen.
Teacher	Good. What if the cost of the ticket was $1?
Tashi	Well, 975 people would attend.

Teacher	How did you figure that out
Tashi	If c is 1 than n equals 1000 minus 2. That's 975 people.
Teacher	How can you use that information to give the number of people who will attend if the cost is $2 per ticket?
Tashi	You just multiply 25 times That's 950 people.
Teacher	Now you are supporting your answer with numeric details.
Tashi	I get it.

The feedback offered by Tashi's teacher enables Tashi to explain and support her answer. The context (concert by the Maxed Out Jumping Beans) offered by Tashi's teacher engages and motivates Tashi.

Productive instruction

Tashi's teacher works with Tashi (and a small group of students) to create a table with information to support and prove the answer. Tashi asks if the group can create a poster to display the information. The students are motivated and engaged in the task. When the students reach $10 per ticket, they ask the teacher how to show that the pattern continues. They add the new information to the bottom of the chart.

Event: Maxed Out Jumping Beans Concert

Algebra: $n = 1{,}000 - 25c$

Cost (c)	People (n)
$ 1	975
2	950
3	925
4	900
5	875
6	850
7	825
8	800
9	775
10	750
⋮	⋮

Final thoughts

Because Tashi's teacher provided academic empowerment with specific interest connections, Tashi was fully engaged in the math lesson. There were no problems with Tashi text messaging or insulting the teacher. In fact, because of the direct intervention and more interesting context, Tashi did not even use the hall pass to check her text messages. She was so involved in the activity that she actually had a brief reprieve from the stress of her family crisis.

Felix the Fighter

Felix displays a host of misbehaviors in his General Math class. He has been involved in several fights this semester. He threatens other students and cuts class often. He has a short temper and often tries to assert dominance over his peers. Today, Felix walks into class, slumps down in a chair (not his assigned seat), pulls his sweatshirt hood over his head, and crosses his arms across his chest. He looks really ticked off. The teacher is afraid to say anything to him for fear that he may explode with anger. The teacher decides to ignore Felix.

Problem Sources: True or False

1. This problem is Felix is an angry young man who needs to be in a special education classroom.

   False. Just because Felix is angry does not mean he needs to be in a special education class.

2. This problem is Felix's parents. They do not show any interest in Felix's education or well being.

   False. Felix's parents do care about him; but they do not know how to deal with his anger.

3. Felix has anger management issues. He does not know how to appropriately express his emotions.

   True. We are not diagnosing a medical condition; rather we are recognizing the fact that Felix has issues with managing his anger. Recognizing these issues, alone, will not solve the problem, rather, it is the beginning of the journey toward a solution.

4. The problem is Felix's peers are afraid of him. The other students need to stand up to him.

   False. Although we do not want our students to have fear in the classroom, having the other students stand up to Felix will most likely provoke a fight, which will not help the situation.

5. The problem is that by ignoring the behavior, the teacher is feeding into a potential explosion of anger.

   True. Even though ignoring Felix is better than challenging him while he is in this state, Felix needs to be acknowledged, supported, and redirected (not ignored).

6. The problem is that Felix is working at a higher level than everyone else in this class. He feels as though he has been placed in the wrong class and wants to try more challenging math material.

   True. To address these issues, Felix needs academic empowerment and emotional empowerment.

Multiple Choice: Which Solution Will Work? A, B, or C

Solution A: Authoritarian rule with humiliation

To solve this problem, the teacher needs to take control of the classroom by embarrassing Felix into compliance. The teacher should make Felix feel guilty about taking the teacher's time and energy with his displays of defiance. The teacher should demand that Felix sit up, take the hood off his head, take out his materials, and STOP wasting the other students' time. If he does these things, maybe he will learn something for a change.

Why Solution A will not work for Felix

Felix responds to shame and embarrassment with anger and violence. This solution fuels the fire and may result in an aggressive altercation. Obviously

Felix is angry. The teacher should not antagonize him. Additionally, the do-this-and-maybe-you-will-learn-something-for-a-change attitude sends the message that the teacher is superior and the student is incompetent.

Solution B: Behavior modification with a reward

To solve this problem, the teacher should use a behavior modification plan that includes a reward. Because Felix likes to decide where he will sit rather than sitting in his assigned seat, the teacher knows that this reward will be meaningful to him. If Felix participates in class without being angry, he may choose where he would like to sit.

Why solution B will not work for Felix

This solution is not a good idea for three major reasons. First, the desired behavior is not clearly defined. "Without being angry" is a phrase that is too ambiguous and gives sole discretion to the teacher to decide if the student will get the reward or not. Effective behavior modification plans must include clearly defined behaviors and be evaluated by the teacher and the student. Second, "without being angry" may be initially unattainable for Felix. Felix is angry often. Does the teacher expect this to change overnight? The teacher should help Felix focus on what to do with his anger, not pretend that he can easily turn the emotion on and off. Felix needs incremental steps to realize the ultimate goal. Third, the reward may or may not work. It is true that the reward seems desirable to Felix, which could serve to temporarily motivate him. But the reward could backfire if Felix sits next to someone that he wants to threaten or if Felix takes the reward even if it is not earned. If the reward actually does serve to change Felix's behavior, the results will most likely be only temporary and a new plan will be needed.

Solution C: Academic empowerment and emotional empowerment

To solve this problem, Felix's teacher needs to address his academic needs and his emotional needs. Felix needs to be taught at his level (not below his level). Felix also needs emotional empowerment that addresses anger management and self-esteem.

Why Solution C will work for Felix

By focusing on Felix's academic and emotional needs, his teacher will help Felix productively engage in the learning process. Teaching Felix some anger management skills and addressing his self-esteem will better prepare Felix to be successful in the classroom environment.

Essay: Emotional Empowerment

Possible strategies for Felix

As with many people, Felix's anger is a response to pain or unhappiness. When Felix is angry at someone, he sees only the things that he dislikes about the person. All redeeming qualities of that person are forgotten, which makes it easy for him to want to harm the person. Felix needs to learn this about himself so that he can begin to address his anger management problem.

To break the emotional habit of anger, Felix should try some strategies that will help him control the anger before it controls him. He could try de-stressors such as deep breaths, counting to himself, saying the alphabet to himself, visualizing a pleasant location, or some other calming technique. After he decides which of these de-stressing strategies seems to be the best fit for him, he can try it and evaluate the effectiveness. With the teacher's help, Felix can learn which de-stressing techniques are the most beneficial for him (and the classroom community).

Many people who anger easily have a low tolerance for frustration. Felix needs to learn how to express his frustration without unproductive anger. He could try prompts such as, "I am frustrated because..." or "It upsets me when..." These prompts and other similar sentence starters help give Felix control of his emotions and allow him to communicate these emotions in a more productive fashion.

Possible strategies for Felix's Teacher

Felix's teacher needs to acknowledge Felix's feelings without propelling his anger. The teacher also needs to offer support or assistance to show that the teacher cares about Felix and wants him to be successful. Finally, the teacher needs to carefully redirect Felix. These three steps, 1) acknowledge, 2) support, and 3) redirect, will help Felix be more available for learning. For example, the teacher may say, "Felix, you look upset. Is there something I can do to help?" When Felix shakes his head to indicate no, the teacher can calmly redirect by stating, "Please take a minute to get ready and then take out your math book." Notice that this is not a question. It is a direction. Yet the teacher empowers Felix and gives him a few minutes to collect his emotions by using the "when you are ready" phrase.

The physical stance of the teacher has significance in this situation. To better connect with Felix, the teacher pulls up a chair to be at eye-level with Felix. The teacher does not want to be too close as to invade Felix's personal space, but close enough to show concern. The teacher should not stand over and look down at the student. The eye-level technique (not to be confused with a combative stare-down) helps defuse Felix's quest for power. It sends the message that the teacher is not trying to overpower Felix, rather the teacher is offering a positive, compassionate connection.

Humor can be a productive strategy as well. Laughter can serve to dilute anger. The teacher should not confuse humor with sarcasm. A sarcastic remark from the teacher about Felix will most likely provoke the anger. However, the teacher could poke fun at herself or tell an unrelated joke to help defuse Felix's anger.

Self-esteem

Self-esteem involves our feelings about ourselves, particularly how we perceive others feel about us. If we feel valued and cared about by others, we tend to have higher self-esteem. Felix does not think others like him or care about him. He thinks the teacher and the guidance counselor who placed him in this class think he is stupid. To protect himself from the unpleasant depths of low self-esteem, Felix tries to dominate others by fighting and threatening or simply opts not to go to class. Although these strategies temporarily protect Felix from feeling low self-esteem, they are unproductive strategies that do nothing to help solve the problem.

There are several things that Felix and his teacher can do to help build Felix's self-esteem. However, general compliments will not work. Non-specific compliments tend to make matters worse because the recipient typically doesn't believe them, thinks the compliments are fake, or doesn't really understand what they mean. Therefore, it is important that all compliments from the teacher, in fact all feedback, are very authentic and specific.

Specific and authentic compliments are often easier to provide when the teacher follows the motto "catch them being good" as opposed to "catch them being bad." When Felix is engaged in learning, the teacher can acknowledge this. When Felix comes to class prepared to learn, the teacher can highlight it. When Felix opts to solve a math problem in an efficient or interesting way, the teacher can emphasize and encourage it. These specific and authentic compliments can be offered either privately or publicly depending on Felix's receptivity to them.

To further build Felix's self-esteem, he needs to work on improving his behavior through incremental steps. We do not want to set him up for failure. Instead, he can make small positive gains. This week, he comes to class each day. Next week, he sits in his assigned seat each day. The following week, he shares how he solved a math problem. Next, he gives an authentic and specific compliment to his teacher or one of his peers. Each step brings him closer to being emotionally empowered in math class.

Another strategy is for Felix to do something positive for someone else. Because Felix knows the math material very well, the teacher could ask Felix if he would consider tutoring one of his classmates or another student after school. This suggestion highlights Felix's math abilities and allows him an opportunity to do something for someone else. Charitable acts make a person feel good and when a person feels good, his self-esteem is more likely to increase. Successful tutoring could help Felix, the other student, and the teacher!

Essay: Academic Empowerment

Formative assessment

Felix's teacher gives him a formative assessment to find out what he knows about the upcoming unit on probability. Specifically, the teacher wants to learn the degree of understanding Felix had about analyzing possible outcomes in probability situations.

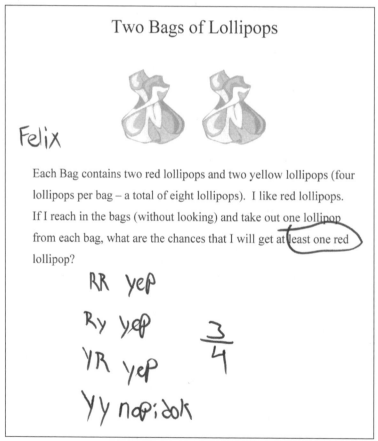

Two Bags of Lollipops

Felix

Each Bag contains two red lollipops and two yellow lollipops (four lollipops per bag – a total of eight lollipops). I like red lollipops. If I reach in the bags (without looking) and take out one lollipop from each bag, what are the chances that I will get at least one red lollipop?

RR yep

Ry yep

YR yep $\frac{3}{4}$

YY nopidok

Note. This problem, "Two Bags of Lollipops," appears in *Family Math Night: Middle School Math Standards in Action*, by J. Taylor-Cox and C. Oberdorf, 2006, p. 69, Larchmont, NY: Eye on Education. Copyright 2006 by Eye on Education. Reprinted with permission.

Felix's response to the formative assessment indicates that he knows a great deal about probability and possible outcomes. He clearly lists each possible outcome (Red & Red, Red & Yellow, Yellow & Red, and Yellow & Yellow) and specifies if each possible outcome contains "at least one red." Felix's use of "yep" to affirm that there is at least one red in the outcome sends the message that he is rather bored with the task. "Nopidok" for "no" is Felix's way of poking fun at the task. The use of these slang words does not minimize the accuracy of his answer, instead it gives the teacher insight on who Felix is and how he is feeling about the task. Because this formative assessment is actually a preassessment, the teacher will need to offer more challenging material for Felix because he already knows the content.

Meaningful feedback

After reviewing Felix's response, the teacher engages in meaningful feedback with Felix.

Teacher	Hey Felix, I was entertained by how you proved your answer with yeps and nopidok.
Felix	(*laughs*) I was just having fun.
Teacher	I thought it was funny and your answers are absolutely correct.
Felix	Yep.
Teacher	(*laughs*) What if we change the probability situation a bit?
Felix	Like how?
Teacher	What if there were more lollipops in each bag?
Felix	Maybe four of each color?
Teacher	Sure. Do you think there is a pattern?
Felix	I think it would be the same answer, if that's what you mean.
Teacher	Why?
Felix	Because you just double the outcomes, but the probability is the same.
Teacher	What if there were two reds, two yellows, and two oranges in each bag?
Felix	And you still want to get at least one red?
Teacher	Yes. And you still only take one from each bag.
Felix	I don't know if it would still be 3/4.

Teacher	How could you find out?
Felix	I could list the outcomes.
Teacher	Try it.
Felix	Does orange count as red since it is made from yellow and red?
Teacher	Ahh. Nopidok.
Felix	(*laughs*). Ok. I'll work on it.

The feedback offered by Felix's teacher in this verbal exchange was humorous, engaging, and productive. The teacher affirmed Felix with some joking around, yet was able to prompt his mathematical thinking. The teacher gave Felix a challenging twist on the problem and Felix actively and independently began to solve the problem.

Productive instruction

The teacher works with Felix and a few other students who are working at a similar level. The teacher displays an equation and asks the students to interpret it. $P = 1/2 \times 1/2$ The students decide that it is easy to solve for P because it involves only multiplying one half by one half. But when the teacher asks the students what it means, they do not know. The teacher presents the idea that P stands for Probability. This hooks the students into the original formative assessment. They know that the probability of the YY (yellow & yellow) outcome was 1/4. Felix explains to the group how each of the other three outcomes (RR, RY, YR) was also 1/4. The teacher helps the students analyze the use of "one half times one half" to describe 2 out of 4 in each bag in the original scenario. The students continue to build conceptual knowledge of how to use and analyze equations to explain probability using different probability situations.

Final thoughts

Because Felix's teacher provided academic empowerment and emotional empowerment, Felix was able to find success in math class. Felix's desire to fight and intimidate other students dramatically decreased because he felt better about himself and his relationship with his teacher. Felix, his teacher, and guidance counselor discussed and planned for Felix's placement in a more advanced math class for the next semester.

Rude Rashanda

Rashanda is angry and rude. She back talks her high school geometry teacher constantly. If the teacher yells at her, Rashanda yells back. Today, while the students were supposed to be working on an assignment, Rashanda was searching through her backpack.

Teacher   Rashanda, stop messing with your backpack and get to work!

Rashanda The work is boring.

Teacher   It is not.

Rashanda It is so!

Teacher   It is not.

Rashanda YES it is! (slams her books on the desk).

Teacher   Don't slam your books.

Rashanda I can if I want.

Teacher   No, you can't. This is MY classroom.

Rashanda That's why I am leaving this F#@&IN' place!

Teacher   Good riddance!

Problem Sources: True or False

1. This problem is Rashanda's fault. If she would fix her bad attitude and stop using foul language, everything would be fine.

   False. Blaming Rashanda does nothing to help solve the problem. Why was she looking through her backpack? Why wasn't she working on the task? The answers to these and other questions will help us begin to solve this behavior problem.

2. This problem is Rashanda's parents' fault. They let her get away with everything. She rules the roost at home.

   False. Rather than blaming Rashanda's parents, we need to help Rashanda learn how to express her emotions appropriately and engage in a respectful relationship with her teacher.

3. The problem is that Rashanda has ODD (Oppositional Defiant Disorder). If she had some medicine and therapy, it would help her.

   False. ODD is a real disorder, but Rashanda does not have it. Rashanda does not need medication.

4. The problem is that Rashanda is constantly performing for her friends. She wants to make everyone gasp when she challenges the teacher and uses curse words.

   True. Part of Rashanda's quest for power and revenge includes making the teacher look bad. Her classmates serve as the audience for this performance. When asked, several classmates expressed that they felt that the teacher "deserved it" because "she started it," indicating that Rashanda has earned the support of some of her peers.

5. The problem is that Rashanda's teacher often initiates confrontation and engages in power struggles with Rashanda.

   True. The teacher initiates confrontation when she yells at Rashanda to "stop messing with her backpack." Actually, Rashanda was finished with her assignment and simply getting a book to read from her backpack. The "Yes it is-No it isn't" debate was a childish struggle for power. The power struggle continued until Rashanda used foul language and left the classroom. The teacher's pursuit of power was so strong that he needed the "last word."

6. The problem is that the curriculum is too easy for Rashanda. She is bright and typically already knows the material the teacher is teaching. The bottom line is that Rashanda is just plain bored in her geometry class.

   True. To address these issues, Rashanda needs academic empowerment and emotional empowerment.

Multiple Choice: Which Solution Will Work? A, B, or C

Solution A: Authoritarian rule with a punishment

To solve this problem, Rashanda should be suspended from school. She needs to be punished for using foul language and leaving the classroom without permission.

Why Solution A will not work for Rashanda:

Rashanda has been suspended from school many times. Punishments are designed to alter behavior. Clearly, Rashanda has not changed as a result of previous suspensions. The punishment is not working. The suspension simply serves as a way for the teacher and administrators to get back at Rashanda.

Solution B: Behavior modification with infraction consequences

To solve this problem, the teacher needs to develop a chart that lists each possible classroom violation and the associated consequences. Rashanda will study the chart and take a quiz on its contents so that she knows all the rules and consequences of the classroom.

Why solution B will not work for Rashanda

The "Infraction Consequences Chart" is a punishment chart serving to feed more power to the teacher. Creating consequences without the person to whom the consequences may apply is not productive. Having Rashanda take a quiz on the infraction chart is a waste of time that will most likely result in making Rashanda angrier and more vengeful.

Solution C: Academic empowerment and emotional empowerment

To begin to solve this problem Rashanda's teacher needs to address Rashanda's academic needs, her social needs, and the teacher's own social needs. Because the work is easy for Rashanda she has too much free time in the classroom. The teacher needs to provide some academic challenges for Rashanda to engage her in learning, rather than struggling with the teacher for power. Rashanda also needs emotional empowerment to help learn how to respect herself and others. The teacher needs to learn how to deal with potential power struggles and learn to engage in mutual respect.

Why Solution C will work for Rashanda

If the teacher teaches Rashanda at her academic level, he will initiate mutual respect and Rashanda will have a more productive experience in class. Academic empowerment is a key ingredient in solving this behavior problem. Equally important, Rashanda's behavior and the teacher's behavior need to change. Social empowerment with a focus on dealing with potential power struggles and earning mutual respect will help resolve this type of behavior problem.

———————◆———————

Essay: Emotional Empowerment

Possible strategies for Rashanda's teacher

The first strategy for the teacher to employ is to ask a question rather than initiate a confrontation when a potential misbehavior is observed. Using a calm, non-accusatory voice, the teacher can ask, "What are you doing?" or "What do you need in your backpack?" or "May I help you find something?" These questions invite Rashanda to explain that she is searching for something to do because she has completed the assignment. Rashanda could actually be complimented for looking for something productive to do, such as read a book.

The best way to deal with a potential power struggle is to avoid it. If the teacher does not engage in the power struggle, there is not a struggle for power. A very successful strategy that can be used to avoid power struggles is to "give the gift of time." The teacher should not take the bait that the student is dangling in front of him. He needs to walk away from the situation and allow Rashanda to get herself together. After things have cooled down, he and Rashanda can discuss the situation in a calm, productive manner. The teacher should ask questions, state his feelings and invite Rashanda to do so as well.

Teachers need to steer clear of arguments. Arguments are the seeds of power struggles. Rashanda thinks the assignment is boring. So it is boring to her. Arguing with her about how the assignment is not boring is a waste of the teacher's time and energy. Imagine how differently the situation would have turned out if the teacher responded to Rashanda's "The work is boring" statement with "It may seem boring to you because you are bright and very capable. Let's add a more challenging component to the task."

Claiming sole ownership of the classroom is dangerous. When the teacher states, "This is MY classroom" he intends to isolate Rashanda. He pushes her away. It is not surprising that she leaves. Although, based on the support that some of the students have given to Rashanda, it is possible that the classroom is more Rashanda's than it is his. Clearly, the most productive classrooms are not yours or mine, but rather "ours" because teachers and students are working together to establish a productive environment.

The teacher needs to abandon the need for the "last word." Saying "Good riddance" when a student angrily leaves the classroom is rude and immature. The teacher is modeling the exact behavior that he does not want Rashanda to display.

Possible strategies for Rashanda

Rashanda needs a plan for what she is going to do when she completes her assigned task. Something math related to do should always be available for Rashanda. An ongoing anchor activity such as a "Geometry

Autobiography" would be beneficial. The Geometry Autobiography is a book about how Rashanda has used geometry throughout her life (each chapter is a specific age and includes descriptions of geometrical concepts, formulas, and theories).

Rashanda needs a way to express her anger without disturbing the teacher or the rest of the students. She can record her feelings in a private journal (unfiltered recordings are permitted if they are not shared with anyone). She can also write the teacher a note (filtered for respect) to express her feelings.

Rashanda needs a consequence for two specific behaviors. What happens if she uses foul language and what happens if she leaves the classroom without permission? She does not need a consequence for being rude because the behavior is too vague and the sole judgment is left to the teacher. She does not need a consequence for arguing, because the teacher is not going to argue with her, so there will not be any arguments. Using foul language and leaving the classroom without permission are two very specific behaviors. These misbehaviors are blatant (obvious to everyone) and inappropriate (disruptive to the teaching-learning process). Whatever the appropriate and understood consequence (e.g., detention, parent meeting), the teacher should state the consequence in a calm manner and resume teaching. This takes the intensity out of the situation and allows the classroom environment to return to a positive state.

Mutual respect

Respect should not be given or demanded. Respect should be earned. Students respect teachers more often when teachers respect students. Respecting someone does not mean being afraid of that person. In fact, fear can dilute or pollute a respectful relationship. Mutual respect involves communicating honestly, being reliable, and building relationships. When potential conflicts arise, teachers and students can use these situations to promote mutual respect by identifying stressors, sharing feelings, negotiating, and working together to solve problems.

Essay: Academic Empowerment

Formative assessment

The assignment that Rashanda worked on in class could be used as a formative assessment. The information gathered from this formative assessment can be used by the teacher to academically empower Rashanda.

Clearly Rashanda understands how to find the surface area of a cylinder. Many of the other students in the class used incorrect formulas to solve this problem (e.g., finding the area of a circle instead of the diameter, multiplying length times height). But Rashanda accurately and efficiently solved the problem with enough time to add a distasteful, yet none-the-less humorous twist to the problem (changing the word sod to indicate that the field would be covered with mucous fluid). Rashanda is bored with the assignment because she already owns this knowledge and clearly needs more challenging material.

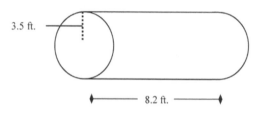

The field crew will press the fresh ~~sod~~ snot on the football field using a cylindrical roller with the dimensions shown below.

3.5 ft.

8.2 ft.

Note: The figure is not drawn to scale

How much area will one revolution of the roller cover? 180 sq ft
Round to the nearest square foot.
Explain and justify your answer.

$C = \pi d$ $3.14 \cdot 7 = 21.98$ $21.98 \cdot 8.2 = 180.236$ Rashanda

Meaningful feedback

Instead of engaging in a power struggle with Rashanda, the teacher could have opted to provide some meaningful feedback.

> **Teacher** Rashanda, I see you have finished the assignment. May I take a look at it with you?
>
> **Rashanda** Sure.
>
> **Teacher** (*laughs*) I don't think I would want to play football on that field!

Rashanda *(laughs)*. I was just kidding (erases the word snot from the paper).

Teacher   How did you know to find the circumference and multiply it by the length of the cylinder?

Rashanda Well, at first I started to find the area of the circle, but then I thought, that's not going to help me. I needed the circumference.

Teacher   How did you explain and justify your answer?

Rashanda That's why I drew the arrow there. The formula and equations are my explanation and justification.

Teacher   That makes sense. How is an explanation different from a justification?

Rashanda I don't know. The both just show how you solved it, I guess.

Teacher   Yes, how you solve it is the explanation. Why you solved it that way is a justification.

Rashanda Oh, I get it. I think I could justify my solution a little more.

Teacher   How?

Rashanda Maybe I could prove how finding the area of the circle and multiplying that by the diameter of the cylinder does not show the surface area.

Teacher   Good idea. After you add that, see if you can come up with a different problem that requires you to use the area of the circle to solve it.

Rashanda OK.

The feedback offered by Rashanda's teacher in this verbal exchange is meaningful. The teacher deals with the "mucous issue" in an effective way. He uses humor and Rashanda has no need to challenge him. She simply erases it from her paper. The teacher affirms Rashanda, teaches her about reasoning and proof, and offers her a follow-up challenge. The teacher respects Rashanda and Rashanda respects the teacher.

Productive instruction

Rashanda's teacher works with Rashanda and a few other students who need more challenging material. Using the same problem scenario (cylinder rolling sod on the football field), the teacher adds an additional component. How many revolutions of the cylinder are needed to cover the entire football field? The students decide that most football fields are 100 yards long, so they try to solve the problem by dividing 300 square feet by 180 square feet (1.6…). Rashanda announces that something has to be wrong. The teacher asks the students to draw a representation of the football field. When doing so, one of the students asks, "How wide is the field? Rashanda laughs and adds, "That's what's wrong. We covered only one little part of the field, not the whole thing!" The teacher asks, "What should we do?" They decide that most fields are about 50 yards wide (150 feet). They multiply 150 by 300 and find 45,000 square feet. The students race to divide 45,000 by 180. One student calls out, "250 square feet!" Rashanda announces, "You mean 250 revolutions!" Everyone agrees.

Final thoughts

The next class period, Rashanda rushes in to talk to her teacher. She shares with him that football fields are actually 120 yards (including the end zones) by 53 1/3 yards. She shares with him how she found the information and re-calculated the number of cylinder revolutions needed to cover the field. In this situation Rashanda has not only engaged in further learning but she has been inspired to challenge herself academically! Her teacher commends Rashanda and asks her if she thinks it would take the same number of cylinder revolutions to cover a Canadian football field. Rashanda smiles and replies, "I don't think so, but I will find out!"

Carlos the Clown

Carlos is the class clown. He acts silly to gain the attention of his peers. He also has a "roaming problem." When he gets a hall pass to go to the rest-room, he is gone for a long time. He likes to walk the halls peeking in classroom windows looking for his friends. Today, Carlos is on his teacher's last nerve. Instead of studying trigonometry, he is dancing around the classroom playing the "air guitar." Many of the other students are beat-boxing (making vocal percussion sounds) to encourage Carlos' antics. The teacher screams, "Shut up!" points at Carlos and yells, "Stop acting like an idiot!" Carlos ignores the teacher, continues his performance, then bows to the class and sits down in his seat.

Problem Sources: True or False

1. The problem is that Carlos is an idiot. He needs to stop acting stupid and get control of his behavior.

   False. Carlos is not an idiot. He is already in control of his behavior. Unfortunately, the behavior he is in control of poses problems in the teaching-learning process of trigonometry (or any other subject, for that matter).

2. This problem is Carlos' parents. They think he is funny.

   False. Carlos' parents are just as frustrated with his behavior as is the teacher. Sometimes they act like they think Carlos is funny to save them from being embarrassed.

3. The problem is that Carlos has Tourette's syndrome. He needs a treatment plan.

   False. Carlos does not need a treatment plan for Tourette's syndrome because he does not have it.

4. The problem is that Carlos' peers propel Carlos' misbehavior.

   True. Carlos enjoys performing for his peers. The positive reinforcement Carlos receives from his peers makes him want to continue entertaining them even though the teacher does not find it amusing.

5. The problem is Carlos' teacher does not know how to channel Carlos' passion for entertainment. The teacher is easily frustrated, overreacts, uses insults, and is unable to provide positive instruction for Carlos.

   True. Screaming "Shut up!" to students and calling a student an idiot is inappropriate and often serves to entertain the students rather than force them to behave. The teacher needs to uncover Carlos' learning preferences and help him use those preferences to learn the trigonometry content.

6. The problem is that some of the trigonometry curriculum is confusing to Carlos. He does not understand and uses comical antics to divert attention away from the content.

   True. To address these issues, Carlos needs academic empowerment and learning empowerment.

Multiple Choice: Which Solution Will Work? A, B, or C

Solution A: Behavior modification with extinction (eliminating reinforcement)

To solve this problem, the teacher needs to implement a behavior modification plan that includes extinction. The student's misbehavior will fade away because the reinforcement (from the other students and the teacher) is eliminated. The student's classmates and the teacher will simply not react to his foolish behavior.

Why Solution A will not work for Carlos

Extinction is a difficult strategy to successfully employ for several reasons. It is a gradual and time-consuming process that often starts with an increase in the unwanted behavior. Carlos will most likely "act up" more often and more intentionally to gain the attention he craves when he realizes that his classmates and teacher are not reacting in the way he desires. Furthermore, it will be difficult, if not impossible, to guarantee that all of the students follow the "simply not react" process. Most likely someone will snicker or otherwise crack, which will serve to reinforce the unwanted behavior, making Carlos all the more resolved to seek further reinforcement.

Solution B: Authoritarian rule with coercion

To solve this problem, the teacher will use coercion to stifle Carlos' misbehavior. The teacher will gain power over the student by causing him anguish. The student will comply because he does not want to experience the discomfort. The teacher is in charge. The teacher will overpower the student using commands and demands.

Why solution B will not work for Carlos

Authoritarian rule with coercion will not work for Carlos because Carlos has learned to use humor as a distraction. If the teacher makes demands, Carlos will make a joke. If the teacher gives a command, Carlos will do something to make the other students laugh. Carlos has perfected the art of humorous distraction. The teacher's coercion will not be effective and will most likely escalate the misbehaviors and consequences.

Solution C: Academic empowerment and learning empowerment

To solve this problem, Carlos' teacher needs to address Carlos' academic needs and his learning needs. Because the work is too difficult for Carlos, the teacher needs to use some scaffolding and intervention techniques to help Carlos gain comfort with the content. The teacher also needs to uncover Carlos' learning preferences, address these preferences, and redirect his creativity to help Carlos learn how to be a successful student. Additionally, the teacher needs to learn how to appropriately and productively respond to Carlos' conduct.

Why Solution C will work for Carlos

By uncovering and addressing Carlos' academic needs, the teacher will help Carlos understand the content and find success. Knowledge of and attention to Carlos' learning preferences will give Carlos the empowerment he needs. Improving the teacher's response to Carlos' misbehavior will also serve to help solve the problem.

Essay: Learning Empowerment

Possible strategies for Carlos' teacher

When a teacher yells "Shut up" or says a student is acting like an idiot, the teacher has lost control. These are desperate, reactive responses that are nonproductive. Many students perceive that the teacher has "lost it." Other, more spiteful students feel that they have "won" when they can provoke such responses from the teacher. Neither of these outcomes serves to benefit the teaching learning process or enhance the classroom environment. The teacher needs to understand the anger and use effective anger management strategies.

It is natural for a teacher to be frustrated with Carlos when he is distracting the class and directing the attention away from the teacher. The problem is exacerbated when the frustration turns to anger. When a person is angry at someone, his opinion of that person becomes negative. The only points of reference are the things that are displeasing about that person. The teacher cannot see the humor in what Carlos is doing. What's more, the rest of the class is involved and encouraging him, making the focus of the anger expand to all that are involved. The teacher needs to understand how this process unfolds and how unproductive it actually is.

A teacher, by controlling his anger, can help a situation in multiple ways. He does not propel the problem, he avoids potential power struggles, and he models to students what to do when they are angry. Basic anger management strategies include recognizing anger patterns and situation triggers, and having effective response plans. Some people find it beneficial to concentrate on something else when they are angry. Perhaps the teacher can think about a vacation spot, a special person, or a pleasant event. Another idea is for the teacher to distract himself by counting, reciting a verse, or recalling a mathematical formula. Thinking about something other than the anger or the object of anger (Carlos) helps the teacher manage the anger in a productive manner. Of course, each person using these strategies needs to find the strategy that works best for him. Evaluating the effectiveness of anger management techniques is critical to the success.

Following the anger management strategy, the teacher needs to utilize an effective response to Carlos' attention-seeking behavior. The teacher should use responses that will help solve the problem. It is acceptable to give Carlos some of the attention that he craves, but we need to do this in a positive way. Clearly, this is not a time for questions such as, "Will you stop? "Do you want to sit down?" "Is your show going to last long?" Instead, the teacher needs to greet, redirect, and offer to help the student. The teacher could say, "Hello Carlos! Please, sit down and take out your textbook. I will be happy to help you get started." Or "Carlos, you bring a smile to my face. It's time to focus on the assignment. I will work through the first problem with you if you want." In these examples the teacher meets Carlos' attempts at humor with pleasantries, specific directions, and an offer of support. The teacher should try to find the phrases that are most comfortable (and natural) for the teacher and the most effective for Carlos.

Possible strategies for Carlos

At some point we would like Carlos to understand why he has the need to inappropriately dance around the classroom or roam the hallways. Learning that these behaviors provide a way for him to escape the difficulties he is having in the class will be a helpful revelation. Yet, simply telling Carlos this information may backfire (making him feel worse and thereby causing him to increase the problematic behavior). Instead, we want Carlos to learn this through successful classroom experiences paired with decreased frequency in his distracting entertainment and roaming.

Ultimately, we want Carlos to know how to gain attention in appropriate ways. Unfortunately, he has had years of experiences doing the opposite. He is hungry for attention and will go to great lengths to get it. One strategy to try is to allow Carlos to earn attention. If he makes specific and authentic attempts to study the content (in whatever ways he and the teacher agree upon), he could earn a five-minute performance for the class. The plan could be referred to as the "Five for Five." Five class periods without outburst or roaming and he gains five minutes of fame to perform for the class. Carlos and the teacher should construct this plan together so that they both know the expectations and outcomes. Initially, it could be five class periods. Then the plan could move to five consecutive class periods. Then maybe performance time is given intermittently. Ultimately, we want to remove the reward and help Carlos find intrinsic motivation. To do that successfully, Carlos should be part of the decision making. The teacher should ask Carlos to help access his achievements and determine when it is time to stop using the reward.

The "roaming the halls looking for friends" behavior should be addressed specifically. Many students who have this issue are attempting to replace unhappy feelings in the classroom with the pleasant emotions found in the hallways. When a person feels unsuccessful, it is natural for the person to want to escape from that emotion. The first step in solving this problem is making Carlos feel successful in class. We want the classroom environment to be such that students do not want to escape from it.

Environmental preferences and multiple intelligences

Carlos' environmental preferences should be addressed. He needs space. He needs to be able to move around when he is working. Instead of sitting at a desk that is surrounded by other desks, he needs to sit on the aisle or in a place that he has room to stretch. He should be allowed to get up and move around with the understanding that he cannot distract others when doing so. When we give students freedom to help address their learning needs and environmental preferences, we empower them to take charge of their own learning. Of course these strategies need to be evaluated for effectiveness. Is it working? Is Carlos successful? Are other students distracted? How can Carlos have the movement and space he needs while successfully participating in class? Carlos should be involved in this evaluation process to help him learn how to do it for himself.

Using a multiple-intelligences survey, Carlos and his teacher learn that he is a "music smart" person. To encourage this intelligence and creativity, Carlos can be invited to create rhythmic chats and raps to help him learn and to show what he has learned. When students are encouraged to use their strengths during the process of learning and as a culminating activity, their motivation and ability to tackle the content increases.

———◆———

Essay: Academic Empowerment

Formative assessment

Using a simple, yet informative formative assessment, the teacher uncovers some of Carlos' academic needs. This formative assessment is a preassessment that allows the teacher to uncover Carlos' misconception and provide productive instruction.

Name _Carlos_

Joe is fishing. While he patiently waits for something to nibble the bait, he thinks
about the angles and sides of the fishing pole and line. The tip of the fishing rod,
angle C, is 91°. The end of the line in the water, angle A, is 28°. The fishing pole,
side a, is 5 feet long. Use the Law of Sines to find the length of the line from the
tip of the pole to the end in the water (side b).

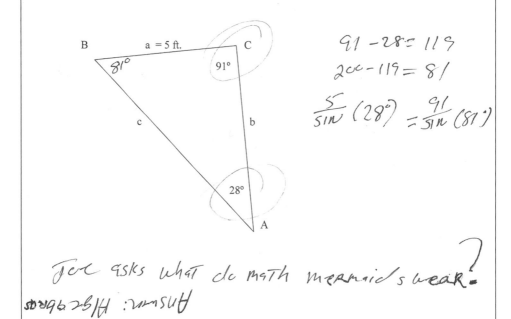

$$91 - 28 = 119$$
$$200 - 119 = 81$$

$$\frac{5}{SIN}(28°) = \frac{91}{SIN}(81°)$$

Joe asks what do math mermaids wear?
Answer: Algae-bras

Carlos' response to the formative assessment reveals some of the misconceptions that he has about how to use the Law of Sines to solve for an
unknown side. Carlos erroneously substitutes 91 for b or what b represents.
Additionally, Carlos lacks foundational concepts about the area of a triangle.
His use of humor about what "math mermaids wear" is an attempt at distracting the teacher's attention from his inaccurate work to the funny riddle.

Meaningful feedback

Rather than focusing on the distraction, the teacher engages Carlos
in meaningful feedback that will address his gaps in understanding and
misconceptions.

Teacher	Carlos, I see you have worked on solving the fishing problem.
Carlos	Yeah.
Teacher	Tell me about how you found angle B.
Carlos	All the angles have to add up to 200 degrees. So I just added and subtracted.
Teacher	It was a good idea to add and subtract. How many degrees in a circle?
Carlos	That's 360.
Teacher	How do you know that?
Carlos	I remember it from when I used to ride my skateboard. If you turn all the way around, that's a 360.
Teacher	Nice connection to your experiences. What if you drew a square inside the circle? How many degrees would the angles of the square be?
Carlos	I guess it is 360°.
Teacher	How could you prove that?
Carlos	The square is inside the circle.
Teacher	What size are the angles in a square?
Carlos	They are all 90°. They have to be.
Teacher	Right.
Carlos	And four times 90 is 360.
Teacher	Yes. Let's draw a square on this paper.
Carlos	OK.
Teacher	Now divide the square into two equal triangles.
Carlos	OK. Done. What's the point?
Teacher	How many degrees in a triangle?
Carlos	It's half of the square, so it is 180°.
Teacher	Absolutely true. All triangles have angles that equal 180°.
Carlos	Oh (looks back at his formative assessment), I used 200. I need to fix that.
Teacher	Yes. And could we send the math mermaids back to algebra class?
Carlos	(laughs). OK. I will.

The feedback offered by Carlos' teacher served to offer Carlos some meaningful ways to connect to the content. He used his background experiences to relate to the foundational concepts needed to work with the Law of Sines. Knowing the total degrees of the three angles in a triangle is an essential piece of knowledge. Now Carlos has ownership of this knowledge because he has a deeper conceptual understanding and the teacher was able to help Carlos see his misconception in a respectful manner.

Productive instruction

Carlos' teacher works with Carlos and a few other students in a small group setting. The goal of the mini-lesson is to help the students understand the relationships among the sides and angles of a triangle so that they can show and apply the Law of Sines.

Using the same fishing pole and line scenario, the teacher asks the students to sketch the triangle on small dry erase boards. The teacher asks, "What do we know about this triangle?" The students call out the angles, and the teacher asks them to add this to their sketches. Carlos adds, "We also know that angle B is 61° because 91 + 28 = 119 and 180 − 119 = 61. The other students agree and include this in their sketches. Another student shares that the length of the fishing pole (side a) is also known and the students include this measurement in their sketches. The teacher asks, "What do we know about the relationships of the angles and sides?" One student responds, "I think you have to set it up with the side over sine times the angle but I don't know why." Other students agree and one shares, "It has to be the same letter. Like little a and big A." The teacher explains, "The Law of Sines involves the ratio of the sine of an angle to the length of its opposite side." Carlos asks, "But why does $\frac{a}{sinA} = \frac{b}{sinB} = \frac{c}{sinC}$?" The teacher replies, "That's a great question! The common value of these three fractions is the diameter of the triangle's circumcircle." One student asks, "What is the circumcircle?" The teacher explains that the circumcircle (also known as the circumscribed circle) of a triangle (or any polygon) is the circle which passes through all the vertices of the triangle (or any polygon). The teacher sketches a diagram of this on his dry erase board. The students ask a few other questions and make some additional observations and connections. The teacher then brings the students back to the original problem by asking, "How can we find side b of the fishing line triangle?" Carlos responds, "We have to use sine angle B, like this." Carlos writes: $\frac{5}{sin(28°)} = \frac{b}{sin(61°)}$. The teacher enthusiastically replies, "Yes. $b = sin(61°) * \frac{5}{sin(28°)}$. The students use their graphing calculators to solve and find that the fishing line from the tip of the pole to the end of the line is approximately 9.3 feet.

Final thoughts

Carlos' teacher uncovered the exact gaps in knowledge and misconceptions that he had related to the Law of Sines. The teacher addressed these specific issues using questioning techniques, diagrams, connecting to background experiences, and small group targeted instruction. Having the students draw the figures and label them helped the students to connect the diagram to the process of the Law of Sines. Therefore, Carlos did not need to misbehave or gain attention by acting silly because he was given the tools and help needed to be successful in this trigonometry lesson. The teacher decided to add some humor of his own at the end of class. He asked Carlos if he knew about "farmer trigonometry." Perplexed, Carlos said that he did not. The teacher replied, "Farmer trigonometry involves swines and coswines." Carlos smiled and said, "That might give me the coswine flu." They all laughed.

Sleepy Susanna

Every time the teacher turns around Susanna is falling asleep. Sometimes she has her head resting on her arm on the desk. Other times Susanna has her head up but her eyes are closed. The teacher has to say, "Wake up Susanna!" or "No sleeping in class, Susanna" several times every class period. The teacher does not understand why Susanna does not sleep on her own  time. AP Statistics is important. If she doesn't stop sleeping in class, she will not have a chance of scoring high enough on the AP Statistics exam.

Problem Sources: True or False

1. The problem is that Susanna needs to get more sleep at home.

   False. Susanna sleeps eight to nine hours every night.

2. This problem is Susanna's parents. They do not know how often she sleeps in class.

   False. It is not Susanna's parents' fault that they do not know how often she sleeps in class. If they do not know, the teacher needs to let them know.

3. The problem is that Susanna has a sleep disorder called narcolepsy. This causes her to fall asleep during the daytime.

   False. While narcolepsy does involve excessive daytime sleepiness, Susanna does not suffer from this disorder.

4. The problem is that some of Susanna's classmates are also falling asleep during class. She sees them sleeping and that makes her fall asleep.

   False. Sleeping is not contagious.

5. The problem is that Susanna's teacher uses a PowerPoint presentation for nearly every lesson. The lights are often dimmed or completely off to allow the students to better see the screen.

   True. The environment is more conducive to napping than it is to learning statistics.

6. The problem is that the AP Stats class is actually quite boring for Susanna. She already knows most of the material, is not a visual learner, and finds it easy to fall asleep when the lights are dim or off.

   True. To address these issues, Susanna needs academic empowerment and learning empowerment (with attention to learning and environmental preferences).

Multiple Choice: Which Solution Will Work? A, B, or C

Solution A: Behavior modification with a reward

To solve this problem, the teacher needs to reward Susanna for staying awake during class. The teacher can give extra credit to Susanna as the reward. She will earn five points for each class period that she stays awake.

Why Solution A will not work for Susanna

Giving extra credit for staying awake during class is a bad idea for several reasons. If the expectation is for students to be awake during class (and one would hope it is), students should not be rewarded for doing so. The teacher needs to figure out why Susanna is falling asleep. The reward itself is also problematic. Susanna is a bright student who is not being challenged. She does not need extra credit for staying awake in class.

Solution B: Authoritarian rule with a punishment

To solve this problem, the teacher needs to punish Susanna every time she falls asleep. The punishment will be detention. Consistency is the key. Susanna will get one detention for every sleeping episode.

Why solution B will not work for Susanna

Detention is a common punishment doled out to students. Unfortunately, it does not work very often. Most of the time the students who are in detention are those who are often in detention—proving that the punishment is not serving to deter misbehavior and is thereby not working. In Susanna's case, falling asleep in class does not merit such a punishment. Moreover, the teacher will not be supervising what happens in detention because the school has a specific detention place and designated monitor. Thus, Susanna may actually fall asleep in detention creating an oxymoronic situation (getting detention for sleeping and then sleeping in detention). Clearly, Susanna's teacher needs to find out why Susanna is sleeping in class.

Solution C: Academic empowerment and learning empowerment

To solve this problem, Susanna's teacher needs to address Susanna's academic needs and her learning needs. Because the work is too easy for Susanna, she does not feel motivated to learn. Additionally, the environment and teaching style are not meeting Susanna's learning needs. The teacher needs to find out what Susanna knows and teach her the things that she does not know about AP Statistics, determining and extending her common knowledge. The teacher also needs to modify the environment, help Susanna uncover and utilize her learning style, and find out why Susanna is sleeping in class.

Why Solution C will work for Susanna

Giving academic and learning empowerment to Susanna will help her stay awake in class. The teacher will academically challenge Susanna and help her to be more available for learning by changing the classroom environment and learning opportunities.

Essay: Learning Empowerment

Possible strategies

The first thing the teacher needs to do is to stop using so many PowerPoint presentations. AP Statistics is an exciting subject. The students need to be more actively involved in the learning. They need to collect, organize, analyze, and interpret data, not just look at slide after slide of various graphs. They do not need to view illustrations of which keys to push on the graphing calculator. Susanna and the students will be more motivated (and less inclined to sleep) if they are encouraged to question, discuss, generate new problems through activity-based instruction, and encouraged to try nontraditional problem solving methods. Simply put, the teacher needs to use more creative teaching techniques.

Additionally, the teacher needs to talk with Susanna. She should ask her why she is falling asleep in class. Susanna may have the courage to tell her teacher that she is bored in class. She may also reveal that "looking at" the screen with the lights out causes her to be tired. The conversation could go a long way in building a positive relationship with Susanna.

During this conversation, the teacher could offer to make some changes and request that Susanna do so, as well. Perhaps the teacher could trim down to using only some PowerPoint slides mixed with times for students to interact with the math content. In exchange, Susanna could try strategies for staying awake in class, such as drinking cold water, standing up, or taking a quick walk around the classroom. The teacher and Susanna should evaluate these strategies to see if they are working or if any revisions or new strategies are needed.

Environmental preferences

Having the lights on more often during class is a needed environmental change for Susanna. Other environmental changes include Susanna moving from the back of the classroom to the front of the classroom. Currently, Susanna sits at a desk in the back. The teacher's view of Susanna (and Susanna's view of the teacher) is somewhat obstructed by a bookshelf. Changing Susanna's seat and adjusting the placement of the furniture will help both Susanna and the teacher monitor the progress of the new strategies Susanna plans to try. With regard to the occasional standing and walking strategies, a specific place and path should be determined so as to cause the least disruption for the other students.

Learning style

A simple learning styles survey revealed that Susanna is not a visual learner. She is actually an auditory learner, which means she needs to talk about the math content and hear others talk about it as well. Verbal exchanges will help Susanna actively engage in learning. Tape-recording portions of the class will also serve to help Susanna use her learning style (and provide experience with a practice that she may want to use later in her college courses). Susanna needs to be aware of her learning style so that she can seek opportunities to learn in this manner. Her teacher also needs to provide opportunities for Susanna to use her auditory learning style in class.

Essay: Academic Empowerment

Formative assessment

Using a simple, yet informative assessment, the teacher finds out what Susanna knows and what she needs to learn. This formative assessment serves as a preassessment for the upcoming area of study.

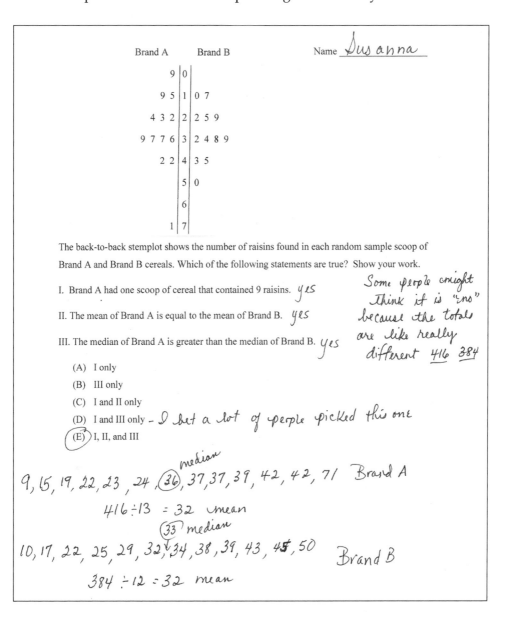

Brand A   Brand B   Name _Susanna_

```
          9 | 0 |
        9 5 | 1 | 0 7
      4 3 2 | 2 | 2 5 9
    9 7 7 6 | 3 | 2 4 8 9
        2 2 | 4 | 3 5
            | 5 | 0
            | 6 |
          1 | 7 |
```

The back-to-back stemplot shows the number of raisins found in each random sample scoop of Brand A and Brand B cereals. Which of the following statements are true? Show your work.

I. Brand A had one scoop of cereal that contained 9 raisins. _yes_

II. The mean of Brand A is equal to the mean of Brand B. _yes_

III. The median of Brand A is greater than the median of Brand B. _yes_

Some people might think it is "no" because the totals are like really different 416 384

    (A) I only

    (B) III only

    (C) I and II only

    (D) I and III only — *I bet a lot of people picked this one*

    (E) I, II, and III

median

9, 15, 19, 22, 23, 24, ㊱, 37, 37, 39, 42, 42, 71 Brand A

416 ÷ 13 = 32 mean

㉝ median

10, 17, 22, 25, 29, 32, 34, 38, 39, 43, 45, 50 Brand B

384 ÷ 12 = 32 mean

Susanna's response to the formative assessment indicates that she is familiar with how back-to-back stemplots (also called back-to-back stem-and-leaf plots) are set up and how to analyze the data. She knows how to find the median and mean in each data set and how to compare the medians and means. She even adds some conversational components to her response. She thinks that some people will not know that the mean of Brand A is equal to the mean of Brand B. She explains that the sums of each data set are "like really different." She even adds that she thinks a lot of people may incorrectly choose answer D because of this. Susanna seems to be "talking about the math" through her written responses. Considering that this formative assessment is a preassessment and Susanna's teacher has not taught stemplots yet, Susanna is going to need more challenging work with stemplots.

Meaningful feedback

Using the formative assessment, the teacher engages in meaningful feedback with Susanna.

Teacher	Susanna, how would you describe the shape of the data?
Susanna	What do you mean?
Teacher	Data can be skewed, symmetrical, bell-curved, or…
Susanna	Oh. I get it. Do you look at one data set at a time?
Teacher	Yes. Figure out the shape of each data set and then compare them.
Susanna	Well. Because of 71 Brand A is kind of skewed. Is 71 an outsider?
Teacher	Are you thinking of outlier?
Susanna	Yes. Outlier. The outlier skews the data.
Teacher	What if we ignore the outlier? What shape are the data?
Susanna	I guess they are sort of symmetrical. And so is Brand B.
Teacher	In this case, we can say that both data sets have somewhat symmetrical distributions, if the outlier in Brand A is excluded.
Susanna	What if the data are not symmetrical?
Teacher	The data may be skewed.
Susanna	So what do skewed data look like?
Teacher	Skewed left is when the left side of the distribution extends much farther than the right side.
Susanna	Skewed right is the opposite, right?
Teacher	Yes.

Susanna	I would like to see some skewed data.
Teacher	I would like for you to work with Marcy (classmate working at a similar level) to create a back-to-back stemplot that has one data set skewed left and one data set skewed right. Talk about it as you work on it.
Susanna	Just make up the numbers?
Teacher	Yes. For this assignment you can. You also need think of what the data are and why someone may want to compare the data sets in a back-to-back stemplot.
Susanna	OK. We will.
Teacher	I also want you to think about the relationship between the median and the mean when the data are skewed right or left.
Susanna	OK.

The feedback offered by the teacher to Susanna in this verbal exchange was meaningful and productive. Susanna learned more about how to describe the shape of the data presented in back-to-back stemplots. She was also given a challenge to work on with another student. The teacher did not want Susanna to work by herself because she knows that Susanna needs to talk about the content to remain actively engaged. The teacher's request that the students think about the relationship of the mean and the median when the data are skewed offers a way for the students to further their conceptual understanding. Susanna and Marcy decided to construct a back-to-back stemplot of girls' and boys' "test scores." Guess which way they skewed the data?

Productive instruction

Using the information from the learning styles survey, the teacher divides the class into groups of students who have the same learning style (visual, auditory, tactile, and kinesthetic). Each group is required to collect data and display the data in a stemplot using the group's learning style. The teacher will give time for each group to collect data from their classmates. As the students begin brainstorming possible data to be collected, the teacher facilitates by moving from group to group answering questions, asking questions, supporting, and redirecting when necessary. The teacher offers suggestions based on the learning style of each group. The kinesthetic group decides to gather data about arm spans and heights. The tactile group decides to collect data about how long it takes each person to put together a simple puzzle. The visual group decides to collect data on how long it takes each student to solve a simple crossword puzzle. The teacher suggests that the visual and tactile groups share data to construct the back-to-back stemplot. Susanna's group, the auditory group, decides to collect data about how many digits of pi can be recited before and after 30 seconds of verbal practice. As they collect the data they begin to notice that the range is small. The teacher shows them how to use a split stemplot to open the data up for further analyses.

After the students collect the data, they work on how to display the data in a stemplot. The visual group makes a poster. The tactile group uses number tiles to display the back-to-back stemplot. The kinesthetic group has people hold digits and stand in the correct place (making a human graph). The auditory group recites the data using changes and accents in voice tone to represent the clusters of data. All of the students were actively engaged in the statistics!

Final thoughts

Susanna's teacher inspired and motivated the students to learn more about stemplots. There were no PowerPoint slides. The lights were on and the environment invited learning. The teacher encouraged Susanna and the other students to use their learning styles to make the content more meaningful. Susanna was given meaningful feedback aimed at exactly what she needed to learn. On her way out, Susanna said to her teacher, "I didn't close my eyes once during class today." Her teacher smiled and said, "Me either!"

Arrogant Anna

Anna acts like the world revolves around her. She is arrogant, talkative, and carries an entitled attitude. Worse still, the teacher suspects that Anna cheated on last week's quiz. Today, Anna is subtly annoying her teacher by swishing the contents of her water bottle around during the calculus exam. When the teacher begins collecting the finished tests, Anna takes out a mirror from her purse and begins fixing her hair. The teacher says, "Now is not the time for that. Please put it away." Anna replies, "Maybe you should try fixing your hair once in a while." The teacher explodes, "Diva does detention today at 3:00!" Anna turns around as if she is looking for the diva who will have detention. The other students snicker. The teacher yells, "You, Anna!" The bell rings and Anna walks out with her nose in the air.

$$\lim_{x \to -\infty} \frac{x^4 + x}{3x^3 + 7}$$

Problem Sources: True or False

1. Anna needs to fix her attitude problem. If she would just stop acting like she is better than everyone else, everything would be fine.

   False. We need to find out what Anna is masking with arrogance. Uncovering these issues will enable the teacher to begin to help Anna be successful in her calculus class.

2. This problem is Anna's parents. They give her everything she wants. She never has to work for anything. They act like she walks on water.

   False. These assumptions about how Anna's parents interact with Anna are not true. Moreover, regardless of how Anna's parents treat her, Anna and the teacher need to work on Anna's classroom behavior.

3. The problem is that Anna has Narcissistic Personality Disorder. Anna would benefit from therapy that addresses this problem.

   False. While Anna exhibits some narcissistic personality traits, she does not have the exaggerated or grandiose views of her abilities associated with Narcissistic Personality Disorder. She does not have the disorder.

4. The problem is that Anna is a snob and has only a small circle of friends. These peers are more like groupies that promote Anna's "rock star" attitude.

   False. Anna's friends are not the reason that Anna misbehaves in school. Anna's attitude is the result of deep-seated insecurities and overwhelming stress.

5. The problem is that the teacher takes the bait offered by Anna to engage in a power struggle. Additionally, the teacher uses name calling and mockery to achieve control.

   True. Although the teacher initially responds appropriately (giving directions to Anna when she takes out the mirror), she lets the insult that Anna gives serve as an invitation to a power struggle. Unfortunately, Anna's teacher displays the exact behavior that she does not want Anna to exhibit.

6. The problem is that the curriculum is too difficult for Anna. She does not understand it and uses arrogance and dishonesty to hide her inadequacies.

   True. To address these issues, Anna needs social empowerment and academic empowerment.

Multiple Choice: Which Solution Will Work? A, B, or C

Solution A: Behavior modification with negative reinforcement

To solve this problem Anna should have detention every class period. If she behaves appropriately in class, the teacher will remove the detention (adverse event) for that day. The goal is to increase Anna's appropriate classroom behavior by removing the detention.

Why Solution A will not work for Anna

Having Anna work to remove daily detention is confusing and unwarranted. Most students view detention as a punishment, not as a negative environmental stimulus to be removed. Anna and her parents will most likely accuse the teacher of being mean and unfair.

Solution B: Authoritarian rule with embarrassment tactic

To solve this problem, the teacher needs to embarrass Anna into compliance. Every time Anna acts arrogant or insults someone, the teacher should belittle her. The constant embarrassment will serve to deter Anna's inappropriate behavior.

Why Solution B will not work for Anna

Anna is already feeling embarrassed due to her lack of knowledge of and confidence in calculus. These are the sources of Anna's displays of arrogance and entitlement. Adding constant embarrassment from the teacher will not solve the real problems.

Solution C: Academic empowerment and emotional empowerment

To solve this problem, Anna's teacher needs to focus on Anna's academic needs and her emotional needs. Because the work is too difficult for Anna, the teacher needs to use some scaffolding and intervention strategies to help Anna increase her comfort and confidence with calculus. Anna also needs emotional empowerment. The teacher needs to help Anna take responsibility for her words and actions. Additionally, the teacher also needs to work on avoiding power struggles.

Why Solution C will work for Anna

Identifying and addressing Anna's academic needs will help build some needed foundations and fill some of Anna's gaps in understanding. Uncovering and working with Anna's emotional needs will give Anna the empowerment she needs to be successful. Improving the teacher's response to Anna's words and behavior will help solve the problem.

Essay: Social Empowerment

Possible strategies

Avoiding power struggles is a key concept when working with difficult, defiant students. When Anna throws the unwarranted insult at the teacher ("Maybe you should try fixing your hair once in a while."), the teacher has several options: 1) The teacher can take the bait and join the power struggle by throwing an insult back at Anna ("Diva does detention today at 3:00!"); 2) The teacher can ignore Anna, pretending as if Anna's offensive statement was not heard; 3) The teacher can give a warning, such as "Anna, you will have detention if you continue to insult me"; 4) The teacher can state the facts, "Anna, insults are not permitted in this classroom"; 5) The teacher can use humor to deflect the potential conflict such as, "I can't look in the mirror because I might scare myself!"

The first two options are not good ideas. Power struggles are not beneficial in the classroom. Name calling and trying to embarrass students do not help build a positive classroom community. Pretending not to hear an insult may avoid the power struggle, but it does not help solve the problem and may, in fact, cause the student to offer more insults. If the teacher hears the insult, chances are that the student and others around know that the teacher heard the insult.

Giving a warning to the student can be helpful. It really depends on how the warning is delivered. If the teacher uses a combative tone or dominant physical stance with the warning, chances are it will been perceived as the second punch thrown in the fight for power between the student and the teacher. To be effective a warning should be calm, direct, and quick. The best warnings simply serve as reminders of known consequences.

Stating the facts is a beneficial strategy to use when working with difficult students. When the teacher says, "Anna, insults are not permitted in this classroom," the statement serves as a reminder to Anna. It also serves to let all of the students who heard Anna insult the teacher know that the behavior is unacceptable. As with the warning, stating the facts needs to be delivered in noncombative, calm, direct, and efficient manner. Most of the time, the teacher should just walk away after "stating the facts." This gives the student time to save face and gives the teacher time to cool down.

Humor, not to be confused with sarcasm, is also a valuable strategy. When the teacher pokes fun at herself, the students are invited to laugh without anyone being insulted. The humor serves to deflect the harshness of the situation and sends the message that there will not be a power struggle. Of course, if the humor is at the expense of the student, the student will most likely perceive it as an insult and the power struggle with be in full swing.

The teacher and Anna need to begin to establish a relationship based on trust where insults are unwelcomed. The first steps involve the teacher proving to Anna that she can be trusted and then inviting Anna into conversation. When Anna is comfortable enough, perhaps she will be able to tell her teacher about the tremendous stress she is under based on the amount of pressure that she feels—the college applications, grades, tests, the SAT scores, and AP exams, everything is piling up and Anna just can't take it anymore. At this point, the teacher needs to support Anna by listening to her and by acknowledging her feelings. The teacher may even be able to suggest some additional supports.

Anna may decide to gain some needed relief from the burden she is carrying by confessing that she cheated on the exam. It will take a great deal of courage for her to admit that she wrote formulas and answers on the inside of the label on the water bottle to use during the exam. If Anna is able to do this, the teacher will, again, have options. The school's administration may need to be involved based on school or district policy involving academic integrity. Should Anna be punished for cheating? Should she fail the test because she cheated? Should Anna be allowed to retake the test because she confessed? How can we best help Anna take responsibility? This is a golden opportunity to build a positive relationship with Anna.

Responsibility

Responsibility involves personal accountability. The goal is for students (and teachers) to acknowledge and accept ownership of what they choose to think, feel, say, and do. If Anna thinks her actions are the teacher's fault (if she would just leave me alone, I won't have to insult her) and if the teacher thinks her actions are Anna's fault (if she wouldn't insult me, I wouldn't have to call her a diva, embarrass her, and give her detention), neither party is being responsible. A responsible person does not blame others for her actions; instead she takes ownership of her thoughts, words, and deeds.

Anna also needs to understand that cheating on the test was not her parents' fault (because of the pressure) or her teacher's fault (because of the content); it was her choice. Gratefully, it was also her choice to admit to the dishonesty. It is good to have something positive to include in this difficult situation. Should the accolades for admitting the dishonesty be equal in magnitude to the consequences for cheating? What are the natural and logical consequences that will help Anna take responsibility and resist later temptations to cheat? The decisions made will have great impact on Anna's future.

Essay: Academic Empowerment

Formative assessment

A formative assessment helps reveal some of the misconceptions or gaps in knowledge that Anna has. The teacher uses this information to target the instruction for Anna, offering her academic empowerment.

Name ___Anna___

Solve the limit.

$$\lim_{x \to -\infty} \frac{x^4 + x}{3x^3 + 7}$$

$$\lim x \to -\infty \frac{x^4}{x} + \frac{x}{x^3}$$

The limit does not exist!!!

Anna's response to the formative assessment is a response that she gives often. She likes to recapture the Eureka-moment from the *Mean Girls* movie by saying "the limit does not exist!" Unfortunately, she does not understand what it means because she has gaps in her knowledge of Limit Laws. Specifically, Anna needs to learn how to use the highest power of x in the denominator and accurately simplify to find out if the limit approaches anything.

Meaningful feedback

Using the formative assessment, the teacher engages in meaningful feedback with Anna.

Teacher	Anna, let's take a look at this problem.
Anna	OK.
Teacher	You have the limit as x goes to negative infinity.
Anna	Yes. But I don't think I have the expression right.
Teacher	What is the highest power of x in the denominator?
Anna	x^3
Teacher	Yes. Let's use it to divide both parts of the numerator and both parts of the denominator.
Anna	Like this? *Anna accurately records* $\dfrac{x^4}{x^3} + \dfrac{x}{x^3}$
Teacher	You have it. Because we are trying to find out if x approaches anything, we need to do the same thing with the denominator and divide it.
Anna	Oh, OK. I get it. *Anna divides by* x^3 *to get* $\dfrac{3x^3}{x^3} + \dfrac{7}{x^3}$
Teacher	Let's keep simplifying.
Anna	So we end up with (x plus (1 over x squared)) over (3 plus (7 over x cubed))
	Anna records $\dfrac{x + \dfrac{1}{x^2}}{3 + \dfrac{7}{x^3}}$
Teacher	Exactly. Now let's analyze it.
Anna	How?
Teacher	*The teacher points to the numerator of the complex fraction.* It has a big number in the denominator.
Anna	And one over a big number will be positive or negative?
Teacher	Whether it is positive or negative, it will approach zero.
Anna	Yes. It is the same thing with 7 over x cubed. It goes to zero.
Teacher	Perfect. So what are we left with?
Anna	Negative infinity divided by 3.
Teacher	Yes. That's equivalent to negative infinity.
Anna	A big negative number divided by 3 is still a big negative number.
Teacher	So in this case you would say...

Anna	The limit does not exist! *(laughs)*
Teacher	*(laughs)* How can we describe with clarity what is happening?
Anna	The limit is approaching negative infinity.
Teacher	Yes! Much better. You did it!

In this verbal exchange, the teacher helps Anna maintain accuracy while she works with the problem. She builds her confidence as she strengthens Anna's understanding of Limit Laws. The teacher gives some information and then asks questions. She encourages and motivates Anna.

Productive instruction

The teacher offers Anna and several other students a small group mini-lesson on the concept of limits. The goal is to help the students build understanding of calculus limits using a geometric perspective. The teacher begins by having the students work with partners to engage in math discourse about how polygons are related to circles. The students use dry erase boards to sketch polygons with various sides. The teacher invites the students to use a different color to show a circle of the same size on each polygon. The students find that the more sides a polygon has the closer it is to becoming a circle. The teacher asks the students to refer to a polygon as x-gon (x being the number of sides) and discuss to create a statement about its relationship to the circle. After some discussion, Anna shares, "As x gets bigger, the x-gon gets closer to being a circle." The teacher affirms Anna's answer and asks, "Could we also say that as x approaches infinity, the x-gon approaches a circle?" The students agree that this is true. The teacher translates the idea further saying, "The limit of the x-gon, as it goes to infinity, is a circle." The students agree. One student asks, "Will it ever get to be a circle?" The teacher replies, "It never will, but it will be so very close." Anna asks, "Is that why we say it approaches?" The teacher answers, "Yes."

The teacher asks the students to think about the sequence associated with $x/(x+1)$. The students begin recording the sequence starting with $x = 1/2, 2/3, 3/4, 4/5, 5/6, 6/7, 7/8, 8/9, 9/10, 10/11, 11/12, 12/13, 13/14,\ldots$ The teacher asks, What is happening to the terms in the sequence? The students respond that the terms are getting bigger. The teacher asks, "What are the terms getting closer to?" The students respond, "One!" Anna says, "The terms are approaching one." The teacher asks the students to talk to their partners about how this idea could be recorded in "calculus language." The students discuss and work together to write

$$\lim_{x\to\infty}\frac{x}{x+1} = 1$$

Anna says, "I really get this now." The other students agree. The teacher asks the students to work with their partners to think about and write a sequence whose terms approach zero. The students begin discussing possible terms. All of the students, including Anna, take the responsibility for the task.

Final thoughts

Anna continued to work on understanding calculus limits. The teacher offered several additional mini-lessons including how the limits look when they are graphed. With each class period, Anna gained foundational knowledge that helped her find success. She took responsibility for her learning. Her arrogant episodes grew less frequent as her confidence in calculus increased. One day later in the semester, Anna joked with her teacher by announcing, "I guess Diva does calculus now!" Everyone laughed.

5

Smart Moves

In conjunction with increasing students' academic, learning, social, emotional empowerment, solving behavior problems in math class involves creating shared classroom expectations, avoiding power struggles, preventing bullying, having a crisis plan, holding class meetings, empowering decision makers, building respect among class members, working effectively with parents, monitoring progress, and making adjustments.

Creating Shared Classroom Expectations

When Ms. Hall first started teaching, she was told that the best classroom rules were written in collaboration with students. In preparation for the first day of school, she gathered her chart paper and markers and titled the paper "Classroom Rules." As she contemplated all of the possibilities, she started to panic. What if the students came up with rules that she did not want? What if they came up with rules that were not good? What if they missed some important rules? She ran to a veteran teacher and shared her fears. "Oh dear," she said, "don't worry about that. You know the rules you want; you just need to get the students to say them." And that's what she did. She knew the rules she wanted:

1. Keep your hands, feet, and objects to yourself.
2. Treat others how you want to be treated.
3. Be on time for class.
4. Be prepared for class.
5. Listen to instructions the first time they are given.
6. Turn your work in on time.
7. Take care of my classroom and materials.
8. No foul language.
9. No gum.

10. No food or drinks (unless authorized by the teacher).

11. No talking without raising your hand first.

12. No getting out of your seat without permission.

13. Be polite.

14. Be helpful.

15. Do not interrupt the teacher.

16. Do not interrupt other students.

Ms. Hall guided, questioned, and suggested until she got the rules she wanted. She posted these in the classroom and considered it a collaborative effort.

Obviously, there are many problems with Ms. Hall's classroom expectations:

- *There are too many rules.*

- *Some of the rules are presented in a negative fashion.*

- *Some of the rules create classroom contradictions.*

- *Some of the rules are redundant.*

- *The rules are inconsistent because some are specific and some are general.*

- *Some of the rules send the message that the classroom belongs solely to the teacher.*

- *Convincing your students of specific rules does not guarantee shared expectations.*

Questions to consider when developing shared classroom expectations:

How do the students feel when there are so many rules?

What is the difference between a rule and a command?

How do students deal with classroom contradictions?

Does redundancy help students understand why a rule is important?

Are general rules better than specific rules? Why or why not?

How do we send the message that the classroom belongs to students and teachers?

How do we create shared classroom expectations?

Having classroom rules is important. The students need to know and appreciate the classroom expectations. Personally, I have only one rule in my classroom: Respect yourself, others, and our environment.

I create shared expectations with my students by discussing what this rule means to them and to me. How do you show respect to yourself? What are some ways to show respect to others? Why should we respect the environment? We describe situations and decide if they are respectful or not. I also share classroom procedures with my students and we talk about how the procedures align with the rule. For example, I do a lot of small group work and I do not want to be interrupted unless it is an emergency. By giving the small group of students uninterrupted time, we are sending the message that learning is important. We are showing respect for the students' learning. Other classroom procedures support the rule. For example, if a student is working on an assignment and needs materials while I am working with a small group, the student should show respect to himself by getting the supplies he needs and continuing the task at hand. He doesn't need to wait until I am available. If he has a question that cannot be answered by anyone else, he could work on something else until I am available. I want students to be productive whether they are working directly with me or not.

The rule is not only for the students. I need to be respectful of myself, others, and the environment as well. For example, when I am working with a small group, I am not going to leave the rest of the class on their own for long periods of time. My job is to set students up for success. I may work with the small group for a while, then leave them with a task so I can take a walk around the room to provide needed support, redirection, or additional challenge for the other students. The goal is to have all of the classroom procedures align with the rule.

Avoiding Power Struggles

A power struggle is only a power struggle if there are two or more people struggling for power.

If you sense a power struggle,

1. Remain calm.
2. Don't engage in the struggle for power.
3. Don't ask the student to do something for you.
4. State the expectation.
5. Offer assistance in a few minutes.
6. Walk away.
7. Return in a few minutes and ask the student if she wants the assistance.

Notice how Jessica's math teacher avoids the power struggle in this scenario:

Jessica   I am not doing this paper.

Teacher   Jessica, you need to complete the assignment.

Jessica   I SAID I AM NOT GONNA DO IT. IT'S STUPID!

Teacher   Jessica, you need to complete the assignment. I know there are some complex parts to the task and I am happy to help you with it in a few minutes. *The teacher walks away.*

Jessica   It is still stupid.

The teacher ignores Jessica's last comment. The teacher knows that Jessica is feeling as if she is stupid because she cannot do the assignment. He gives Jessica (and himself) a few minutes to cool down. When he returns he helps Jessica with part of the assignment. He does not refer to the previous exchange.

Preventing Bullying

A bully causes pain to someone by harassing, degrading, threatening, stealing, taunting, and/or physically harming. We should teach students what bullying is and that bullying is not acceptable. We need to establish schoolwide consequences for bullying.

If you see bullying, stop it immediately.

1. Name it. "This is bullying."
2. Remind students that it is not acceptable.
3. State the consequence.
4. Do not ask questions of anyone (including bystanders).
5. Do not embarrass the victim.
6. Follow-up:

   ✓ The consequence is part of the process of accepting responsibility.

   ✓ Talk with the bully about how to stop the bullying behavior. Remember, most bullies are dealing with personal insecurities. Many have been bullied themselves.

   ✓ Privately talk with the victim and give helpful strategies (walk away, use humor).

   ✓ Talk with the bystanders about what to do the next time they witness bullying.

   ✓ Let other key educators know about the situation.

   ✓ Inform parents, if appropriate.

Having a Crisis Plan

Even though no one wants a classroom crisis, everyone needs a crisis plan. Crisis plans help us keep everyone safe in times of potential danger. Find out your district's policy. Many schools have established crisis plans. Typically, a crisis plan is imposed when a student is in danger of harming himself, others, or the environment.

A Crisis Team commonly includes at least four adults. The adults use proximity to surround the student. The team leader gives the directions to the student in crisis. The directions are given one step at a time. All members of the crisis team need to remain calm. Physical restraint is the last resort. SAFETY is the goal—for the student in need, for the other students, and for the teacher. The student in crisis needs to relocate. If this is not possible, the teacher needs to take the other students out of the room. Crisis intervention should be performed only by a trained and approved Crisis Team.

Teachers need to make sure they do not abuse the crisis plan. Teachers should not call the Crisis Team for help when they can take care of the situation themselves. For example, if a student writes on the desk, the teacher should not call the Crisis Team because the "environment is in danger." When teachers constantly call upon someone else to resolve behavior issues, they send the message that they are incapable of handling the classroom. However, if an angry student throws a chair across the classroom, for example, the teacher should call the Crisis Team because the safety of everyone is in jeopardy.

Holding Class Meetings

Class meetings are a great way to build community, empower students, and solve problems. Class meetings give students the forum to share what is on their minds related to the classroom. Successful class meetings have an agenda and allow for each person who wants it to have uninterrupted time to share.

When I first began using class meetings, I held a meeting only when there was a problem. Unfortunately, the message I sent to my students was that the class meeting was a punishment. When I realized this, I added "class meeting" in my bi-weekly plans.

The agenda for the class meeting is developed over the previous week. I keep the agenda on a clipboard in the classroom. The agenda is separated into four sections: Compliments, Updates, Issues, and Potential Solutions. Students may add to the agenda at any time during the week. Originally, I allowed agenda items to be added anonymously. But I learned that it was more meaningful for students to claim issues. Everyone shows respect to others during the meeting. We do not interrupt or put down another person's idea. Sometimes the students come up with ideas and potential solutions that I would not have thought of on my own. We hold to time limits during the meeting, unless we all agree that we will give a particular issue more time. If the issue is unresolved, we may put it on the next agenda to give us more time to think of potential solutions.

Empowering Decision Makers

To become good decision makers, students need to engage in making decisions. They need practice identifying and analyzing situations, options, and potential outcomes. They need models for how to compare options and potential outcomes. They need to learn how to reflect, analyze, and modify choices as necessary.

Here are seven steps to good decision making:

1. Understand the situation/issue.
2. Understand the goal/s.
3. Understand the options and potential outcomes.
4. Compare the options and potential outcomes.
5. Make the best choice given the circumstances.
6. Reflect on the choice.
7. Analyze alternatives and modify choice if needed.

Building Respect Among Class Members

How can the teacher expect students to do something that the teacher does not choose to do? Teachers and students respect one another when they consider each other's thoughts, needs, and feelings. To show respect to students, ask them how they feel, affirm their feelings, understand their feelings, show empathy, consider their feelings, and make future decisions based on their thoughts, needs, and feelings.

Some students do not know how to be respectful because their experiences with respect involve power and fear, rather than happiness and satisfaction. It takes time, demonstration, and experience for some students to learn what mutual respect is and how to participate in it.

Working Effectively with Parents

Parents need to know four things: 1) You care about their child; 2) You know what you are doing; 3) What they say to their children matters; and 4) The subject may look different from when they were in school.

Parents play a major role in the education of their children. From the early learning years through higher education, parents' perspectives, attitudes, and behaviors influence the education of students. We need to *teach parents* how to help enhance the growth of content knowledge, experience, and application in our students.

In my opinion, there are several critical points that teachers should share with the parents of the students they teach. First, let parents know you care about their child—and mean it! Most parents are (and should be) their child's biggest advocate. Most parents want the best for their children because they care deeply for them. We need to teach students (and their parents) what is appropriate and help them understand our expectations. When we work together with parents, we need to be sure that parents know we genuinely care about their children. This helps us work together toward the same goals.

Second, let parents know that you know what you are doing. As the teacher, you are the expert. You are highly qualified to provide instruction. You know what the students need to learn and how they learn. Our goal is to set students up for success. When the work is too difficult, students may become frustrated and shut down. When the work is too easy, students may become bored and disruptive. We want just the right combination of support and challenge to engage students in learning and prompt further learning. Academic empowerment is a highly effective way to implement the balance between support and challenge.

Third, let parents know that what they say to their children matters. Students need to know that their parents appreciate and use mathematics. If a student hears a parent say, "I was never good at math," or "I hated algebra when I was in school!" the student may come to have the same feelings about mathematics. Likewise, if a student hears a parent say, "Math is so important!" or "Geometry is fun!" the student will be more likely to learn to value and enjoy the subject matter.

Fourth, parents need to understand that some things in education may have changed since they were in school. For example, traditional math instruction often involved pages and pages of equations to solve; however, math classes of today are more "hands-on" oriented and students may have fewer, yet more complex and contextual problems to unravel. The goal is to help students apply mathematics thinking to situations to gain a more comprehensive knowledge base in mathematics.

To successfully teach parents how to enhance the growth of content knowledge, experience, and application in our students, we need to send influential messages through our words and actions:

♦ I care about your child

♦ I know what I am doing

♦ What you say to your child matters

♦ The subject may look a little different now

While these ideas do not represent an all-inclusive list, they do offer us a few ways that we can work effectively with parents.

> *Note.* This information comes from the article "The gavel: Parents play a major role in mathematics education," by J. Taylor-Cox, 2006, *The Banneker Banner, The official journal of the Maryland Council of Teachers of Mathematics*, 23(2), p. 1. Copyright 2006 by the Maryland Council of Teachers of Mathematics. Reprinted with permission.

When contacting parents

♦ Contact with good news at least as often as you call with bad news.

♦ Be respectful of their time and yours. Ask when would be a good time for a conversation about their child. Give optional times and optional modes of communication, for example, telephone, face-to-face meeting, email, or text).

♦ Involve the student, if appropriate.

♦ Give at least one positive characteristic or behavior you know to be true about the child.

♦ State the issue in nonjudgmental way.

♦ Explain the consequences or options.

♦ Discuss potential solutions.

♦ Listen to and validate the parent.

♦ It is ineffective to put down the student or blame the parents.

♦ It is inappropriate to give names of other students involved.

♦ Create an action plan.

- Decide how the action plan will be shared with the student.

- Decide how the plan will be monitored and the points of evaluation.

- Set a follow-up date and format.

- Document everything.

Monitoring Progress and Making Adjustments

Solving behavior problems in math class is an ongoing process. Potential problems can appear in any class because we are all human. Students make mistakes. Teachers make mistakes. The thing that matters is how we deal with those mistakes and how we learn to change our behaviors to avoid the same mistakes the next time we are in a similar situation.

We need to monitor academic progress, learning progress, social progress, and emotional progress for each of our students. We need to constantly assess all facets of the empowerment triangle. Major and minor adjustments are needed along the journey toward success. If a student is frustrated, we need to provide instruction that helps build that student's knowledge. If a student is bored, we need to provide instruction aimed at that student's academic level. Using formative assessments, meaningful feedback, and productive instruction academically empowers students and accurately addresses (and ultimately avoids) many behavior problems. We can further work toward solving behavior problems by using learning styles, multiple intelligences, and environmental preferences to strengthen each student's learning empowerment. Likewise, establishing a positive classroom community, using effective and constructive communication, and employing conflict resolution techniques when necessary offer social empowerment and work to solve behavior problems. Moreover, building students' emotional empowerment through increasing self-esteem, taking responsibility, and engaging in mutual respect solves behavior problems.

Clearly, these solutions are not one-time-only strategies. Providing academic, learning, social, and emotional empowerment is an ongoing process that must be monitored by teachers and students; yet monitoring is not enough—our responses to the information we learn as we monitor progress are critical. If a strategy or situation is not working, we need to change it. Continual reflection, evaluation, and responsive action related to the four ways to empower students are the keys to solving behavior problems in math class. Students must be part of the evaluation process.

Final, Final Thoughts

The student scenarios included fourteen students in fourteen different classrooms, ranging from kindergarten to high school. While the situations presented were grade-level-band specific, misbehaviors in the classroom are not tied directly to grade level. Students of any grade level can manifest these or similar misbehaviors. The solutions may need to be tweaked based on the grade level differences, but the underlying mechanisms for solving these problems remain similar. The goal is to empower students. Teachers can do so by focusing on academic, learning, social, and emotional needs.

While this book addresses many misbehaviors that can occur in the mathematics classroom, there are numerous others that can manifest themselves. If you are dealing with a specific problem that is not addressed in this book, you are invited to visit my website (www.Taylor-CoxInstruction.com) and share your situation. We can work through some possible strategies to try and ways to evaluate these strategies. You are not alone. Together we can solve behavior problems in math class!

References

Adler, A. (1930). *The education of children*. Chicago: Gateway.

Adler, A. (1938). *Social interest: A challenge to mankind*. London: Faber & Faber.

Covey, S. (1990). *The seven habits of highly effective people: Restoring the character ethic*. New York: Fireside.

Dreikurs, R. (1948). *The challenge of parenthood*. New York: Duell, Sloan, & Pearce.

Dreikurs, R. (1958). *The challenge of child training*. New York: Duell, Sloan, & Pearce.

Dreikurs, R. (1972). *Coping with children's misbehavior: A parent's guide*. New York: Hawthorn Books.

Dubelle, S. (1995). *Student self-discipline: Helping students behave responsibly*. Rockport, MA: Pro-Active Publications.

Dunn, R., Dunn, K., & Price, G.E. (1985). *Learning styles inventory (LSI): An inventory for the identification of how individuals in grades 3 through 12 prefer to learn*. Lawrence, KS: Price Systems.

Dunn, R., & Griggs, S. A. (Eds.). 2000. *Practical approaches to using learning styles in higher education*. Westport, CT: Bergin & Garvey.

Gardner, H. (1983). *Frames of mind*. New York: Basic Books.

Gardner, H. (1993). *Multiple intelligences: The theory in practice*. New York: Basic Books.

Gardner, H. (1999). *Intelligence Reframed. Multiple Intelligences for the 21st Century*. New York: Basic Books.

Glasser, W. (1965). *Reality therapy*. New York: Harper & Row.

Glasser, W. (1969). *Schools without failure*. New York: Harper & Row.

Glasser, W. (1985). *Control theory*. New York: Harper & Row.

Glasser, W. (1986). *Control theory in the classroom*. New York: Harper & Row.

Glasser, W. (1990). *The quality school: Managing students without coercion*. New York: Harper & Row.

Herzberg, F. (1966). *Work and the nature of man*. Cleveland, OH: World.

Kauffman, J., Mostert, M., Trent, S., & Hallahan, D. (1998). *Managing classroom behavior: A reflective case-based approach*. Needham Heights, MA: Allyn & Bacon, A Viacom Company.

Kohn, A. (1993). *Punished by rewards: The trouble with gold stars, incentive plans, A's, praise, and other bribes*. Boston: Houghton Mifflin.

Kohn, A. (1996). *Beyond discipline: From compliance to community*. Alexandria, VA: Association for Supervision and Curriculum Development.

Maslow, A. (1970). *Motivation and personality.* New York: Harper & Row.

Nolte, D. L. (1998). *Children learn what they live: Parenting to inspired values.* New York: Workman Publishing.

Patterson, G. R., Reid, J. B., & Dishion, T.J. (1992). *Antisocial boys: A social interactional approach.* Eugene, OR: Castalia.

Sears, W. & Sears, M. (1995). *The discipline book: Everything you need to know to have a better-behaved child from birth to age ten.* Boston: Little, Brown and Company.

Skinner, B. F. (1953). *Science and human behavior.* New York: Macmillan.

Slee, R. (1995). *Changing theories and practices of discipline.* London: Farmer Press.

Taylor-Cox, J. (1999). *An exploratory case study of the formal and informal discipline policies used in selected elementary school classrooms.* Dissertation submitted to the Faculty of the Graduate School of the University of Maryland, College Park in partial fulfillment of the requirements for the degree of Doctor of Philosophy.

Taylor-Cox, J. (2006). The gavel: Parents play a major role in mathematics education. *The Banneker Banner; The official journal of the Maryland Council of Teachers of Mathematics, 23*(2), 1.

Taylor-Cox, J. (2009). *Math Intervention: Building number power with formative assessments, differentiation, and games, Grades 3–5.* Larchmont, New York: Eye on Education.

Taylor-Cox, J. (2009). *Math Intervention: Building number power with formative assessments, differentiation, and games, Grades PreK–2.* Larchmont, New York: Eye on Education.

Taylor-Cox, J., & Oberdorf, C. (2006). *Family Math Night: Middle School Math Standards in Action,* p. 69. Larchmont, NY: Eye on Education

Thorndike, E. L. (1913). *Educational psychology. Tome 2. The psychology of learning.* New York: Teachers College Press.

Woolfolk, A. E., & McCune-Nicolich, L. (1984). *Educational psychology for teachers.* Englewood Cliffs, NJ: McCutchan.

Wu, S. (1980). *The foundations of student suspension.* Report to the National Institute of Education.